D0343633

enemies at the gate

enemies at the gate

English castles under siege from the 12th century to the Civil War

Julian Humphrys

ENGLISH HERITAGE

First published 2007 by English Heritage, Kemble Drive, Swindon SN2 2GZ

10 9 8 7 6 5 4 3 2 1

English Heritage is the Government's statutory advisor on the historic environment.

ISBN: 978 1 905624 26 3
Product code: 51243

Edited and brought to press by Adele Campbell
Designed by Doug Cheeseman
Indexed by Alan Rutter
Colour reproduction by F E Burman
Printed in Dubai by Oriental Press

Contents

Picture Credits

All images are © English Heritage/NMR except where indicated below. Reconstruction artists: Peter Dunn, Ivan Lapper, Alan Sorrell. Air photography by Skyscan. Every effort has been made to identify copyright holders and we apologise in advance for any errors or omissions which we will be pleased to correct in future editions.

Siege *n.* the offensive operations carried out to capture a fortified place by surrounding it and deploying weapons against it.

Collins Dictionary and Thesaurus, 1987

Introduction

A s a brief foray into any bookshop will confirm, when it comes to British military history sieges have, on the whole, received considerably less attention than battles. I should add that I have contributed to this imbalance – my first three military historical works have all been about battles and battlefields. There are good reasons why the analysis and description of battles has so occupied the minds of writers and researchers. Winston Churchill famously commented that 'battles are the punctuation marks of history', and some engagements – Hastings, Bosworth and Naseby come to mind – have had an enormous impact on the political development of this country. Yet, as I hope this book will show, sieges were far from unimportant. By the early 19th century the main objective of a European general was more often than not the destruction of his opponent's army, but in earlier times this was less often the case. In most medieval and early modern conflicts the capture of fortified places was a vital part and, often, the chief aim of a campaign. During his invasion of northern England in 1174, William the Lion's main efforts were directed towards the capture of castles. The Barons War of 1215–16 was primarily one of sieges in which the successful defence of Dover Castle proved a turning point. While Henry V will always be remembered as the victor of Agincourt, it was his mastery of siege warfare and his expertise in the use of artillery that enabled him to conquer Normandy. In 1513 King James IV of Scotland seems to have been much keener on capturing castles than fighting battles. And while the civil wars of 1642–51 were primarily decided on the battlefield, the attack and defence of fortified places normally occupied more of a mid-17th-century English soldier's time than fighting battles ever did.

So, by taking a look at 500 years of siege warfare in England I hope to be able to redress the balance a little. This book examines both the development of fortifications and the techniques used to capture them, and takes a close look at the impact of siege warfare on a number of England's most fascinating castles. Clearly castles could, and did, serve a number of functions – as homes, administrative centres, prisons, status symbols and places in which to entertain. But the key characteristic they all shared was their capacity, in varying degrees admittedly, to resist attack, and this aspect of their history is examined in this book. The individual stories of the many towns and cities that have also been besieged at some time in their history is beyond the scope of this work, but I have referred to some of them in order to illustrate particular aspects of siege warfare. One of the most rewarding things about studying castles is the fact that so many of them can be visited. All the castles examined in detail in this book are easily accessible and many are superbly presented and interpreted, so readers have the enormous benefit of being able to go and see for themselves the site of many of the remarkable events described.

The sieges are presented in chronological order and the castles featured cover the whole country, in the south from Cornwall to Kent, and north to Northumberland. Each one has something to tell us about this fascinating aspect of warfare in which engineering skills, powers of persuasion, patience and the ability to stay healthy and fed were often as important at fighting ability alone. William the Lion's invasion of the north of England in 1173–74 offers some insight into the strengths and weaknesses of castles of that period. Under a determined leader, and stocked with sufficient supplies, many castles could hold out against a besieger who lacked siege artillery. However, they could do little to prevent an invader from ravaging the country around it. The events of 1215–17 show how the inability to capture one castle – Dover – was a key factor in the failure of Louis of France's bid to replace John as king of England. During that war, the sieges of Rochester and Dover proved the vulnerability of castles to mining and, in the case of Rochester, underlined the limitations of the great tower or keep as the key part of a castle's defences. Fifty years later the powerful defences of Kenilworth were strong enough to take whatever Henry III's army could throw at them and, in the end, it was the two great enemies of a garrison – hunger and disease – that led to the castle's surrender. Surviving documents relating to the siege also provide us with ample evidence for the vast logistical operation that was involved in supplying a besieging army.

The 15th-century Wars of the Roses were unusual for their time as they primarily involved the elimination of rivals rather than the control of territory; as a result, sieges were comparatively rare during the wars. The exception to this was in the far north of England, where proximity to Scotland and a sensitive political situation meant that control of castles was absolutely essential. The three years after the great Yorkist victory at Towton in March 1461 saw many of the region's castles change hands with a rather bewildering regularity. On many occasions castles were captured after their defenders decided to change sides, but the fall of Bamburgh in 1464 shows the growing importance of a devastating new factor – gunpowder. James IV of Scotland's capture of Norham in 1513 underlines the point. The English were confident of holding the castle, but James's mighty siege guns made short work of its medieval walls and Norham rapidly surrendered

The impact of gunpowder led to fundamental changes in the construction of fortifications and a separate chapter is devoted to these but, as the events of 1642–51 graphically demonstrate, the medieval castle was far from finished as an instrument of war. By this time few castles could have stood up to a sustained bombardment by modern siege artillery, but such guns were relatively few and far between and it was only in the second half of 1645 when the Parliamentarians were able to concentrate their resources that Royalist castles and garrisons surrendered in great numbers. As a result, many castles saw their most sustained military action at a time when, technically at least, they were obsolete. Edmund Ludlow's defence of Wardour is a case in point. A few large guns would have rapidly battered the castle's flimsy defences into submission but none was to hand, and Wardour held out until it was forced to surrender when the besiegers reverted to the age-old tactic of undermining its walls. Ludlow's fascinating account of his experiences at Wardour illustrate another aspect of siege warfare – the game of bluff and counterbluff that could occur when terms of surrender were being discussed. Beeston Castle rapidly surrendered following a daring Royalist attack in 1643 and the subsequent fate of its governor demonstrates that anyone who surrendered a castle too quickly at that time did so at his peril: he was court-martialled and shot. The castle, which then served as an outpost of Royalist Chester, was later besieged by the Parliamentarians and recent archaeological investigations have helped us understand more about conditions there at the time. During the Civil War, Corfe Castle underwent two eventful sieges, fighting off an attempted storm in the first before falling to treachery in the second. As the castle was defended by a woman, Lady Mary Bankes, both sieges attracted considerable attention at the time, and this book also takes a look at some of the other women who found themselves having to defend their homes. The siege of Goodrich in 1646 saw the use by the besiegers of perhaps the most terrifying weapon of the period – the mortar. *Roaring Meg*, as it became known, caused extensive damage to the castle but its garrison, all hard-bitten Cavaliers, were undeterred and only surrendered when a combination of mining and gunfire brought one of Goodrich's towers crashing down around them. Pendennis was the only one of the castles in this book that was built in the age of gunpowder. Strengthened by extensive earthwork fortifications it would have been extremely difficult to take by storm, and the Parliamentarians elected instead to blockade it by land and sea and starve the defenders into submission.

Contemporary accounts are clearly a valuable source in the study of sieges. They can supply the background information that places a siege in its political and strategic context, explain the plans and intentions of besiegers and besieged, suggest what happened where, list some of those who took part, and provide a sequence of events. They also give us the human detail that brings these sieges to life, whether it is the Scots' disastrous attempts to use a catapult at Wark, the mocking of the Archbishop of Canterbury by the defenders of Kenilworth, or the acrimonious correspondence between besieger and besieged at Beeston. Contemporary sources are quoted throughout the book and because of their importance several are presented more fully as appendices. These illustrate many aspects of siege warfare and include an account of the daring Scottish capture of Roxburgh in 1313; the price paid by the garrison of Bedford Castle in 1224 when it failed to surrender when it had the chance; details of the cost of the siege of Kenilworth through extracts from the Liberate Rolls of 1266; early use of gunpowder in the 14th-century siege of Breteuil; a Parliamentarian account of the Royalist attempts to breach the walls of Gloucester in 1643; Lucy Hutchinson's vivid description of the storming of Shelford in 1645; and the articles of surrender for Pendennis – a masterpiece of loose-end tying by experienced soldiers which is worth comparing with the rather perfunctory terms accepted by the defenders of Beeston. In all cases, spelling and grammar have been modernised where it helps the understanding of the text.

As I have already suggested, one of the great things about having an interest in castles and sieges is the fact that you can explore many of the sites and often stand on the very stones where the action happened. It hardly needs mentioning that a visit to a castle can really help to imagine the events that took place there and understand the strengths and weaknesses of its location, even when damage caused during the sieges themselves, deliberate demolition or 'slighting' after the Civil War, and later additions and rebuilding mean the castle has changed considerably since the siege. This book concludes with some information about visiting a number of key castles.

It is a pleasure to thank the many individuals and organisations that have given me help during the writing of this book. I would particularly like to thank the staff of the British Library, Cambridge University library, the English Heritage library, and the National Army Museum reading room, for their courteous and efficient help. It is impossible to name all the English Heritage staff who over the years have enthusiastically helped me to explore the castles in their care, but I must mention Tracy Borman, Emily Burns, Lisa Hampton, Jon Hogan, Rob Richardson and Alysha Sykes. Thanks are also due to Tish Hickson in the English Heritage plans room, Jonathan Butler and Javis Gurr in the English Heritage photo libary, Doug Cheeseman for his first-rate design work, and above all to my editor, Adele Campbell. Her diligence, flexibility, professionalism and sense of humour have made writing this book an absolute delight.

I would also like to thank Dan Snow for his generous input, Alison Weir for her encouragement and advice, and Brena Roche of Brookland Travel for her help in organising my trips as lecturer on the English Heritage 'Tours Through Time' programme. These trips have proved a wonderful opportunity to explore England's castles in the company of like-minded people – English Heritage members – whose ideas and questions have been so useful in helping me to get the most out of a visit. Finally, affectionate thanks are due to my family; to my parents for introducing me to the delights of barbicans and battlements, and to Catharine, Sarah and James for their love and support – and for cheerfully tolerating the towers of books and ramparts of paper that always seem to spring up throughout the house whenever I undertake a writing project.

Julian Humphrys
April 2007

chapter one

The development of the English castle

Although a few castles had been built by Normans who had settled in the country during the reign of Edward the Confessor, it was the period after the battle of Hastings that saw the first great surge in castle building in England. Defeat at Hastings cost Saxon England its best chance of repelling the Norman invasion, deprived it of its most effective leaders and handed the strategic initiative to William. Yet it would still take nearly five years of tough, brutal campaigning to subdue the English. With perhaps as few as 10,000, soldiers William was faced with a hostile population of two million, periodic rebellion, Welsh and Viking raids and, towards the end of his reign, the very real threat of a Scandinavian invasion. In these circumstances the widespread construction of castles was to be a major factor in the Normans' success in conquering and holding the country. Castles served as bases for military operations, as refuges in the event of rebellion, as administrative centres and as symbols of Norman dominance. One 12th-century chronicler commented that at the time of the conquest, 'in the lands of the English there were few of those fortifications which the French call castles; in consequence the English, for all their martial qualities and valour, were at a disadvantage when it came to resisting their enemies'.

Archaeological evidence suggests that over 500 castles of a variety of shapes and sizes were built during the reign of William the Conqueror. Although some were 'ringworks' – enclosures defended by ditch, bank and palisade – the majority were of the motte-and-bailey type, consisting of a conical earthwork called a motte surrounded by a bailey, an enclosure defended by an earth bank topped with a wooden stockade. Although such castles were relatively quick to build, as indeed they had to be given the dangerous military circumstances that necessitated their construction, their mottes were more than just simple mounds of earth. They were constructed from layers of material – flint, sand, chalk, stones – as well as the soil flung up from the ground upon which they were built. The top of the motte was enclosed by a timber palisade inside which stood a wooden tower. These varied from simple buildings raised up on posts to elaborate affairs of more than one storey. Clearly timber defences had their drawbacks when it came to resisting attack, not least their vulnerability to fire. But building in stone took time and the outnumbered Normans needed their castles in a hurry. Furthermore, trying to erect a stone building on top of earthworks which had not been given time to settle was a recipe for disaster.

Nevertheless, although timber castles continued to be constructed in England until well into the 13th century, by the 12th century many castle builders who had the money replaced their wooden defences with stone. Obviously stone was much more resistant to both bombardment and fire and, unlike wood, did not need to be regularly replaced.

The most notable development of this period was the construction of great stone towers or keeps. Although they are popularly seen as the typical 'Norman' fortification, only the great keeps of Colchester and the Tower of London seem to have been constructed in the reign of William the Conqueror; most were built during the reigns of his successors. The first two Henrys spent huge sums of money building keeps at Norwich, Rochester and Dover and many of the country's leading nobles followed suit, with equally impressive keeps being erected by Geoffrey de Clinton at Kenilworth and Aubrey de Vere at Hedingham. Keeps such as these were not only more defensible than the wooden towers that many replaced but were also impressive status symbols providing improved accommodation for their owners. Although they came in a variety of shapes and sizes, and varied in height from two to five storeys, most were square or rectangular in plan. They were normally entered at first-floor level via a flight of external stairs which were frequently enclosed within a forebuilding to provide additional security and, as at Castle Rising in Norfolk, an impressive ceremonial entrance. A keep's walls could be extremely thick – at Dover over 20ft thick in places – and were often mounted on a splayed base to strengthen the building against undermining, deflect missiles and allow objects dropped from the roof to bounce out into the faces of attackers. Many keeps featured a partition wall built across the middle of the tower. This helped to support the roof and had the added advantage that if, as at Rochester, an attacker managed to get into one side of the building, the defenders could fall back and carry on their defence from the other. As great towers were considered to be too weighty to be built on existing mottes, some builders created 'shell keeps', replacing the wooden palisade on the summit of a mound with a stone wall and constructing lean-to timber buildings against it. Excellent examples of shell keeps can be seen at Farnham in Surrey, Pickering in Yorkshire and Carisbrooke on the Isle of Wight.

But while the stone keep was clearly an improvement on its timber predecessor, the only form of defence it offered was a passive one. Other than dropping stones or shooting from the roof or from loopholes in the walls there was little the defenders could do to prevent besiegers from undermining the keep or bringing up siege engines to bombard its walls from close range. As a result, by the end of the 12th century military architects were looking for ways to enable defenders to strike back. This produced a shift in emphasis away from the keep and an increased reliance on the walls surrounding it. These were made higher to make them harder to scale, to make missiles lobbed over them by besiegers' catapults more likely to miss the buildings inside, and to ensure that stones dropped from the battlements would strike their targets with greater velocity. In addition, projecting towers were placed at intervals along the walls. These were initially square in shape but as time went on they increasingly became rounded, which improved the tower's field of fire, deflected missiles more effectively and ensured there were no vulnerable cornerstones for an attacker to dislodge. Mural towers such as these enabled the defenders to direct flanking fire against the enemy and also shoot down onto any attackers who had succeeded in gaining a foothold on the battlements.

For missile fire such as this, the weapon of choice nearly always seems to have been the crossbow. Whilst a crossbow was considerably slower to load than a normal bow, its range, accuracy and penetrative power made it the ideal weapon in a long, drawn-out siege. History is full of examples of besieging commanders being picked off by crossbowmen. Richard the Lionheart was mortally wounded by a crossbow bolt before Chalus in 1199; Eustace de Vesci, the brother-in-law of Alexander I of Scotland, is said to have been shot in the head by one at the siege of Barnard Castle in 1216; and in 1377 the French are reported to have abandoned the siege of Carisbrooke after their commander was shot dead by a crossbowman as he rode round the castle. Indeed, if Matthew Paris's account of the siege of Rochester is to be believed, King John came very close to meeting the same end as his brother. Having spotted the king in the open and within range, a rebel crossbowman asked permission to try a shot – only to be told by his commander that God alone had the power to take a king's life. To give defending bowmen as clear a field of fire as possible, walls and towers were pierced with a variety of arrow loops: at Dover the polygonal Avranches Tower, which was built in the 1180s, features over 50 loops in two tiers. Most bowmen, however, shot at their enemies from the battlements or the tops of towers, sheltering behind crenellations. Crenels (gaps in the top of a castle wall through which bowmen could shoot) were often fitted with wooden shutters which could be raised to allow a defender to shoot and then swung shut to provide him with cover as he reloaded. A vulnerable section of castle wall might also be fitted with a timber hoarding or brattice – a covered platform that overhung the battlements – allowing defenders to drop missiles onto anyone sheltering at its base. None survive, although the sockets for the supporting beams can be seen in many castles including Rochester and Prudhoe. In some cases, for example at Carisbrooke, timber brattices were replaced with permanent stone structures called machicolations. As a castle's wooden gates were potentially its weakest spot, the most heavily defended part of a castle was normally the gatehouse. By the mid-13th century many were virtually miniature castles in themselves, flanked by towers and often protected by a barbican – an outer defensive work designed to protect the approaches to the gatehouse and funnel any attackers into a narrow killing zone.

This new form of 'active' defence found its fullest expression in 'concentric' castles where an inner circuit of curtain walls and towers was surrounded by an outer circuit of lower walls. Not only did this provide an attacker with an increased number of obstacles to overcome, it also meant that an enemy could be subjected to missile fire from both sets of walls at the same time. Both Dover and the Tower of London were developed into concentric castles but the first castle in the British Isles to be built from the start in the concentric form was Caerphilly in Wales, which was begun in 1268. Another great concentric fortification is Beaumaris, the last of a series of castles built to cement Edward I's hold on north Wales.

It is sometimes said that castle building went into a decline in the later Middle Ages, but this is slightly misleading. In addition to their military roles castles had always fulfilled social functions, serving as residences, administrative and entertainment centres and status symbols. Fourteenth- and 15th-century castle building saw a shift in emphasis away from the military towards these social functions, as England was a largely peaceful realm at this time (with the exception of the northern Marches, where fortified tower-houses continued to be built throughout the period). Owners could therefore invest in luxury rather than security. John of Gaunt spent a fortune on a magnificent great hall at Kenilworth, and at the end of the 14th century the Earl of Northumberland built a new keep at Warkworth, not as a last refuge in the case of attack but as a symbol of his power – the whole castle is adorned with spectacular representations of the family's heraldic devices – and as a highly impressive place in which to live and entertain. A number of new castles were constructed but, like Sir Edward Dallingridge's Bodiam, Lord Hastings' Kirby Muxloe and John Lovel's Wardour, they were primarily built to showcase the power, prestige and taste of their owners. They may have sported all the latest defensive features, but it is clear that these were added as much for show as for any serious military purpose. The entrance to Wardour, for example, was defended by a projecting stone gallery or machicolation, but immediately below it are two large, elegant and decidedly unmilitary windows designed to let light into the great hall. Wardour might have kept a band of marauding peasants at bay but it would have stood little chance against a determined, well-equipped enemy.

But, then again, it was never intended that it should.

chapter two

Siege warfare in the Middle Ages

S
ieges were expensive affairs, and they could also be costly in time and
lives. As a result, if a leader was able to acquire a town or castle through
non-military means such as diplomacy, bribery or treachery, then so much
the better. Henry II received a huge windfall in 1175 when William the Lion
of Scotland was forced to give him the castles of Berwick, Jedburgh,
Edinburgh, Roxburgh and Stirling as part of the price of his freedom after his
capture at Alnwick the previous year. In 1217 Louis of France is said to have
offered the counties of Norfolk and Suffolk to Hubert de Burgh in an
unsuccessful bid to get him to surrender Dover Castle. Margaret of Anjou
handed Berwick over to the Scots in 1461 and promised them Carlisle in
exchange for their support against Edward IV, and was herself to gain castles
through treachery on a number of occasions in the next couple of years.

More often than not of course it required force – or at least the threat of
force – to take an enemy castle. Unless a commander was planning to launch
a surprise attack upon a castle he would normally commence proceedings by
calling upon its garrison to surrender. If the garrison agreed, they could expect
to be allowed to march out unmolested, often taking their weapons and equipment with them. However, if they refused, and the attackers were forced to
mount an assault, the garrison's lives and property were technically forfeit if
the castle fell. In practice, further negotiations often took place during the
course of a siege with the surrender terms being offered depending on the
situation at the time. Sometimes, for example at Carlisle in 1174 or Stirling in
1314, a garrison might agree to surrender if it was not relieved by a certain date.
Hostages would be exchanged to ensure compliance and the castle would be
left alone until the given day. But it was not unknown for commanders to

renege on their word. In 1152 John Marshal, who held Newbury Castle for Matilda against King Stephen, secured such a truce by handing his 5-year-old son William over to the king as a hostage. Despite making such a personal investment he then broke the terms of the truce by resupplying the castle and refusing to surrender. When he was told that his son would be hanged and his body catapulted back into Newbury, Marshal is said to have called Stephen's bluff, commenting that he still possessed 'the hammer and the forge to produce another'. The boy was spared – and grew up to be one of the greatest knights in the realm. If contemporary chroniclers are to be believed, garrison commanders often announced their intention to fight on with a noble or stirring speech, but on occasion a summons to surrender was met with insults or scorn. It is said that when William of Normandy appeared before the gates of Alençon in 1051 some of the townspeople mocked the humble origins of his mother, a tanner's daughter, by hanging hides over the ramparts. Predictably, William was not amused and when he captured the town he showed what he thought of the joke by lopping off the hands and feet of 32 of its inhabitants. Alençon's castle still held out but when the amputated hands and feet were thrown over its walls its horrified defenders rapidly surrendered. Indeed, when they were faced with a stubborn garrison, besiegers sometimes resorted to methods that hardly conformed to romantic notions of medieval chivalry. In 1139 King Stephen captured the illegitimate son of the Bishop of Salisbury, brought him in chains to the gates of Devizes and threatened to hang him unless his mother, who was holding the castle, agreed to surrender. She did.

At the other end of the spectrum to the formal summons was the surprise attack. Under Robert Bruce in the early 14th century, the Scots excelled at this hazardous activity, partly out of necessity as they were so short of siege equipment. Issued 50 years earlier, the statutes of Dover Castle show just how seriously the threat of a surprise night attack was taken. The first five read as follows:

I   At sunset the bridge shall be drawn, and the gates shut; afterwards the guard shall be mounted by twenty warders on the castle walls.

II   Any warder found outside the walls, or otherwise off his guard, shall be put in the donjon prison, and punished besides in body and goods at the constable's discretion...

III After the last mount, two sergeants shall turn out of their houses to serve as chief guards. They shall make continual rounds within the castle to visit the warders on the walls and see that they right loyally keep their watch without going to sleep...

IV It is established by ancient rule that if a chief guard discover a warder asleep, he shall take something from him as he lies... or cut a piece out of part of his clothes, to witness against him in case the warder should deny having been asleep, and he shall lose his day's wage, viz 2d.

V And if it happen that the sergeant will not make such arrest, for pity's sake... then he shall be brought before the constable, and be sentenced to prison 'dur et fort', after which he shall be led to the great gate in the presence of the garrison, and there be expelled from the castle...

However, in the early 14th century the garrisons of Edward II's castles in Scotland do not seem to have been so careful. In 1312 the Scots staged a daring night attack on Berwick, using rope ladders with wooden rungs and hooks designed to grip the parapet of the city wall. They were only foiled when the sleeping garrison was roused by the barking of a dog. Linlithgow was captured when soldiers were smuggled into the fortress in a cartload of hay, which was then used to jam open the castle's gate. In 1313 Perth fell to a night attack led by Bruce himself, who had waded with his men across the castle's moat. The following year Sir James Douglas took Roxburgh Castle at night after disguising his men with blankets – it is said that the garrison mistook the advancing Scots for a herd of cattle! The English used similar tactics during the Hundred Years War in 1437 when troops camouflaged with sheets surprised and captured Pontoise by crossing the frozen River Oise at night, then scaling the walls before the defenders could react. Scaling ladders could also be used in a set-piece siege, although the troops climbing up them were horribly exposed to the countermeasures of the defenders who would attempt to push the ladders away from the battlements and, as well as shooting at their enemies, could drop a variety of unpleasant things onto the men below. If the wind was favourable, quicklime could be released to blind the attackers and, though boiling oil was rarely if ever used, heated water and red-hot sand were frequently poured down from the battlements. A wise commander would try to dilute the effectiveness of the defenders' response by attacking in several places at once while his archers and crossbowmen, often operating from the shelter of wattle hurdles (thousands were used at Kenilworth), would unleash a barrage of arrows and crossbow bolts in an attempt to keep the defenders' heads down.

Siege towers offered a less exposed way for attackers to reach the battlements of a castle. Sometimes known as belfries, these wooden behemoths had walls of wood and wattle and were divided inside into several floors connected by ladders. As they needed to be at least as tall as the wall they faced, siege towers could be of considerable height. In 1147 the English built two such towers for the siege of Lisbon, one 95ft and the other 83ft high. Some siege towers, like the one constructed at Bedford in 1224, were static contraptions designed to enable the attackers to shoot over a castle's walls. Others were mobile: fitted with wheels or rollers, they were designed to be pushed or hauled up to the castle wall where a rudimentary drawbridge could be lowered from the tower to enable the soldiers sheltering inside to swarm across onto the battlements. Before a siege tower could be brought into action the attackers had to level the ground and make sure it was firm enough to bear the tower's weight. It was not unknown for defenders to dig pits in front of a vulnerable section of wall then refill them with soft earth so that an approaching tower would sink into the ground. Ditches and moats also needed to be filled. An account from Lanercost Abbey, the *Lanercost Chronicle*, mentions Scottish attempts in 1315 to fill the moat at Carlisle with fascines – bundles of wood and sticks – while at the siege of Jerusalem in 1099 a penny was offered to any man throwing three stones into the ditch in front of the city. Such preparations and the slow speed with which the towers were manoeuvred into position must have given the defenders a reasonable amount of time to prepare for their arrival. At Damietta in 1169 and Carlisle in 1315 the defenders used the time to heighten the threatened section of wall by constructing wooden towers of their own. In 1081 the Byzantine defenders of Dyrrachium also built a tower and when the Norman belfry approached they pushed out a large wooden beam to prevent its drawbridge from being lowered. Although at Kenilworth in 1267 a siege tower known as *the Bear* seems to have been destroyed by stones shot from the defenders' catapults, the main enemy of the wooden belfry was fire. An approaching siege tower would become the target of a variety of projectiles – fire arrows, burning faggots, heated stones and bolts, and jars of 'Greek fire' (a highly flammable mixture of resin, pitch, sulphur, naphtha and oil) – all designed to set it alight. As a result, most towers would be covered with a variety of materials to protect them from fire. Freshly slaughtered hides and felt soaked in vinegar or urine were often used, while at Acre in 1189 Richard I covered his tower in sheets of metal. Despite such precautions, siege towers frequently fell victim to fire – as the crusaders discovered to their cost in their wars against the Muslims who were expert pyrotechnicians. The defenders of Tyre in 1111 destroyed a Frankish siege tower by setting up a horizontal beam along which they winched buckets of burning oil, tar and wood. During the Seventh Crusade two more Frankish towers were burned to the ground – together with the men inside them – by Greek fire, launched by the defenders of Damietta. Nevertheless, siege towers also had their successes. Three were used by the crusaders in the capture of Jerusalem in 1099 and in 1301 Edward I had a prefabricated belfry made in Glasgow and delivered to him on 30 carts for the siege of Bothwell. Moved towards the walls on a road of logs, its use led to the fall of the castle after a siege of just three weeks.

If the attackers were unable to go over a castle's walls their other option was to create a breach and go through them. Before castle walls were built of stone this could simply be done by the use of fire; one section of the Bayeux Tapestry clearly shows two Norman knights setting fire to a wooden palisade on the motte at Dinan. In 1111 the soldiers of Louis VI tried to capture the rebel castle of Le Puiset by pushing carts full of wood smeared with pig fat up to its wooden gatehouse. Their intention was to use the wood to burn down the gate but they were driven back by a hail of missiles. In the end they came up with a simpler solution: they hacked their way through the castle's palisade with axes. Even when stone had replaced timber, castles still remained vulnerable to fire. Although the tower of Brough Castle was built of stone there was enough wood inside it for the Scots to set it alight and force its surrender in 1174. Indeed, fire remained a constant danger to a castle whatever its walls were built of. Its baileys would have been crammed with any number of wooden buildings – stables, storehouses, breweries, granaries – and the Constable's Tower at Dover still houses a long metal hook that was used to pull down burning thatch from the roofs of such buildings and thus prevent fire from spreading. Gates, of course, were always built of wood and the primary purpose of the 'murder holes' often found in the masonry above them seems to have been more to allow water or sand to be poured down to extinguish fires started by the enemy than to enable unpleasant materials to be dropped on attackers.

Attackers might attempt to batter their way through a wall or gate using a ram. A contemporary text describes one constructed for the Bishop of Besançon during the siege of Acre:

It is usually called a ram, because it destroys the solid fortifications of the walls like the ram by repeated and rapid blows. The bishop ordered to apply the ram, which was strongly covered on all sides with pieces of iron, to destroy the walls... He brought the ram, which resembled a vaulted house, to breach the walls. Inside was a huge mast whose head was fitted with iron. The ram, pushed by many hands against the wall, was swinging back only to strike again with a greater force. And so they tried by repeated blows to hollow out the side of the wall or breach it and those who swung the ram and struck it continuously were well protected inside from any possible damage from above.

In fact, despite its armour, the bishop's ram was eventually destroyed when huge stones dropped from the battlements smashed through its iron roof. Defenders might also attempt to nullify the effects of a ram by lowering large pieces of timber or mattresses of straw and cotton to absorb the effects of its blows. In 1216, during the Albigensian Crusade, the French defenders of Beaucaire Castle succeeded in ensnaring a ram in a noose and also lowered down a sack of burning sulphur, which drove off the attackers with its noxious fumes. At Tyre in 1111 the Muslim defenders used a rope with a large hook to catch a ram that was housed on one of the Franks' belfries. Concerned that the defenders might cause the whole tower to topple over by hauling on the rope, the Franks were forced to jettison the ram. During the siege of Ludlow in 1139 the defenders employed a hook for a different purpose. Swinging out a crow – a form of gigantic fishing rod – they succeeded in catching Prince Henry of Scotland who was accompanying King Stephen on an inspection of the castle's defences. In the end only the quick actions of the king prevented Henry from being hoisted to an uncertain future inside the castle.

In practice it was often impossible to use a ram. Such devices were obviously most effective against wooden gates or doors, but these were often either sited at the top of a flight of steps where there was no room to deploy a ram, or simply too heavily defended. After the siege at Dover of 1216–17, for example, an enemy wanting to attack the castle's new main gate would have had to endure flanking fire from a number of mural towers before he got anywhere near the gate, which was itself defended by a deep ditch, a drawbridge and no less than six towers of its own. Furthermore a ram could not be used against a wall built on steeply sloping ground or protected by an unfilled ditch, while the presence of a postern gate might allow the garrison to rush out and over-whelm the ram's operators unless it was closely guarded by soldiers who then themselves became targets for the defenders. Indeed, as curtain walls became stronger and improvements in design enabled the garrison to mount a more active defence, it became increasingly likely that a ram would be put out of action before it could do its job.

As a result, besiegers tended to prefer to cause damage from a distance, employing a variety of catapults to hurl missiles either at or into a castle. The rather imprecise and inconsistent terminology used by contemporary chroni-clers makes it somewhat difficult to identify exactly what kind of catapult was being used. For example, a petraria was clearly a stone-thrower but exactly how it worked is not known, while a chronicler might well describe all siege engines as mangonels. Generally speaking, however, before cannon came on the scene, siege artillery can be divided into three types, working by tension, torsion and leverage respectively. The commonest form of tension machine was the ballista or springald, a giant crossbow that launched massive darts. The defenders of Carlisle are said to have used them with great success against the Scots in 1315. The best known torsion machine is said to have been the mangonel. Like a Roman *onager* it derived its power from a twisted skein of rope, hair or leather wrapped around a horizontal beam. The throwing arm, which is usually described as being fitted with either a cup or a sling to house its projectile, was fixed at right angles to this and pulled back to the ground. When it was released the torsion in the skein would cause the arm to shoot forward to strike a padded crossbar, at which point the missile, normally a stone, would be released. Interestingly machines such as these are hardly ever shown in contemporary illustrations. This may have been because they were so common-place that they were considered less interesting than other forms of catapult. On the other hand they may have been much rarer than we think or not even used at all.

The third type of siege engine, usually called a trebuchet, relied on leverage and seems to have been invented by the Arabs and then adopted by the crusaders. It is virtually the only type of catapult to be shown in contempo-rary illustrations. The earliest form, which was operated manually, consisted of a long wooden throwing arm with ropes at one end and a sling at the other, pivoted between a pair of uprights. Teams of up to 250 men would haul on the ropes so that the arm and sling would pivot upwards and release the missile. However, the end of the 12th century saw a significant technological development. Instead of relying on the muscle power of men, a larger trebuchet would be fitted with a massive counterweight in the form of a box filled with stones, sand, earth or lead. During Edward I's 1304 campaign in Scotland many churches had their roofs stripped to provide lead for such counterweights. Most illustrations show that the box was hinged, thus ensuring that its contents did not spill when the throwing arm was released and also enabling the trebuchet's operators to adjust the weapon's range by altering the amount of ballast in its box. As large machines are said to have been able to lob a 100lb ball over 300yds their operators could work in relative safety, out of the range of a castle's archers and crossbowmen. Really large engines were often given dramatic names. Louis brought *Malvoisin (Bad Neighbour)* to Dover in 1216 while Edward I unleashed *Warwolf* against Stirling in 1304. Such machines took a long time to build – the construction of *Warwolf*, for example, kept 55 men busy for three months. When it was nearly completed the Scots in Stirling asked for terms but the king refused to let anyone leave the castle before he had demonstrated the effectiveness of his new weapon. It was only after *Warwolf* had brought down a section of wall that he allowed the Scots to surrender. Such siege engines were made to be dismantled but even so they were much too large to be dragged round England on campaign. Instead they were stored in various castles around the country and sent for when required. For the siege of Kenilworth Henry III ordered machines to be brought to him from Somerset, Dorset, London and Windsor, while others were constructed with components delivered to the royal camp. Many castles also had their own artillery. Simon de Montfort had ensured that Kenilworth was well provided with catapults and in the late 13th century Pevensey certainly had one for surviving accounts show that it was cleaned and given a canvas jacket in 1290.

Trebuchet stones were often chosen with care. Ideally they had to be hard enough not to fragment when they hit the castle wall although this was of less importance if the intention was simply to destroy buildings and cause casualties within a fortress. During the siege of Newcastle Emlyn in 1287 the English collected 480 stones from the shore below Cardigan and transported them for 12 miles, first by boat up the River Teifi and then by land on 120 carts and packhorses. Stones weighing an astonishing 600lbs have been found in the ditch of the Syrian castle of Sahyun, shot by Saladin's siege engines in 1188. But sometimes a trebuchet's ammunition was of a very different nature. In 1422 Price Coribut of Lithuania launched the bodies of dead soldiers and over 2,000 cartloads of manure into Carolstein in a bid to spread disease among the defenders and it was not unknown for besiegers to fire the severed heads of prisoners into castles. Jean Froissart relates that in 1340, during the siege of the English fortress of Auberoche by the French, an English messenger was captured and sent flying back into the castle with his letters tied around his neck.

While these mighty siege engines clearly had the potential to be extremely destructive, castle walls were built to take a lot of punishment. Froissart relates that during the Hundred Years War defenders often liked to mock their enemies by taking off their hats or pulling out cloths and derisively dusting a wall whenever it was hit by a stone. Furthermore, although catapults were extensively used at the great sieges of Rochester, Dover, Bedford and Kenilworth, there is no evidence that they caused any significant damage and they seem to have been used primarily to harass the garrisons. In fact, during this period the most certain way to breach a stone wall was to cause a section of it to collapse by undermining its foundations. The simplest method of doing this was for a party of miners to hack away with pickaxes at the base of the wall, often under the cover of moveable sheds variously called penthouses, sows or cats. Needless to say both the sheds and the men they protected became the target for whatever the defenders could shoot or throw at them and might also be attacked by sorties from the castle. As a result the favoured method, if the ground was not too hard or wet, was to start a mine some distance from the wall, preferably hidden from sight, and then tunnel towards the target. The roof of the mine would be propped up with timbers and once the foundations of the wall were reached a large cavity would be excavated, shored up and then filled with combustible material. When this was set alight the supporting timbers would burn through and, with no support, the wall would come crashing down. Sometimes a garrison would be aware that a mine was approaching. They might spot its entrance from their battlements, hear the miners at work, see the spoil from the mine or conclude that digging was taking place when they saw ripples in jars of water that they had placed for this purpose at regular intervals along the walls. At this stage, as they did at Dover, the defenders might dig a tunnel of their own in a bid to intercept the enemy's mine, although there was always a risk that this might further weaken the foundations of the wall. Sometimes the defenders would build a makeshift barricade inside the wall that was about to collapse and wait for the inevitable. Often they would surrender. As it was obviously preferable to capture a castle undamaged, it was not unknown for the besiegers to invite its commander to inspect a mine once it was completed and offer him and his men the choice of mercy if he surrendered there and then, or death if he forced them to bring down the wall. A garrison would have to be extremely confident, or desperate, to fight on at this point because once an assault was launched there was no guarantee they would be offered quarter; even if a commander was inclined to be merciful his troops might well ignore his orders, especially if they had suffered heavy losses in the assault.

Although assault techniques have inevitably attracted more attention, the commonest way of capturing a medieval castle was to surround it and starve it into surrender – a course of action that was often adopted when a normal assault had failed. An army that was settling down for a long siege would normally fortify its camp, digging ditches and erecting palisades to prevent it from being raided by the besieged garrison and to protect it against any relief force that might arrive on the scene. Siege engines might be dug in and hundreds of hurdles set up to provide cover for the besieging soldiers. Additional security might be provided by the construction of earth and timber fortifications. Earthworks dug 400yd from the castle during King Stephen's siege of Corfe still survive today. At some of the larger sieges, like Dover, so many temporary buildings were erected that the besiegers' camp came to resemble a small town. Edward III's camp outside Calais in 1346 had 'streets' of shops and even a market place. However, as a tactic attempting to starve a garrison into submission was not without its drawbacks. Operations elsewhere might have to be suspended while an army was involved in a siege. Feudal levies who had served their allotted time had to be paid to stay with the army, while giving mercenaries large amounts of money to sit around doing nothing was not necessarily the best use of a commander's funds. Furthermore, as the royal accounts for the siege of Kenilworth vividly demonstrate, feeding a large army as it sat outside the walls of a castle was a major logistical challenge. As a result it was not uncommon for castles to hold out until relief came or, as happened at Dover in 1216, the besieging force simply gave up and went away. Nevertheless, if a siege lasted long enough and no relief arrived, even the best-victualled castle would eventually be forced to surrender.

Sometimes, for example at Rochester and Kenilworth, although the garrisons were ultimately forced to surrender through lack of food (coupled with disease in the case of the latter) the besieging forces tried to bring things to a more rapid conclusion by continuing in their attempts to storm the castles. On other occasions the besiegers seem to have been content to wait for hunger to have an effect. In September 1142 King Stephen led his army to

Oxford in a bid to capture the Empress Matilda, his rival for the throne, who had established herself in the castle there. Oxford Castle was thought by contemporaries to be particularly strong, and when Matilda's soldiers saw the king's men on the far bank of the Thames they subjected them to a barrage of arrows and insults from the safety of its walls. Goaded into action, Stephen swam across the river at the head of his troops who stormed into the city and set it alight. After building a siege-work to the north of the castle and posting troops around it, Stephen settled down and waited for the defenders to starve. Even though the weather was worsening he does not seem to have made great efforts to assault the castle. He did bring up some siege engines with which to bombard the place but this seems to have been more to lower the garrison's morale than to breach the castle walls. After a relief force under Brian fitz Count had failed to get through to Matilda, her ally Robert of Gloucester tried to lure Stephen away from Oxford by laying siege to the important harbour town of Wareham. He allowed the commander of its garrison to send a message to Stephen saying that he would surrender if the king did not come to his aid within a certain time. Stephen did not move. Wareham surrendered and Portland and Lulworth soon followed suit. Still the king maintained his relentless blockade of Oxford. As Christmas approached and supplies began to dwindle, Matilda played what Roger of Wendover calls a 'woman's trick' on Stephen. On a snowy night she slipped out of the castle with three or four companions and, cloaked in white, made her way unnoticed through the royal lines, eventually reaching her castle at Wallingford. With Matilda safely away, the hungry garrison felt able to surrender and the king granted them generous terms.

Although Stephen had begun his blockade of Oxford in September, the ideal time to start a siege was early to mid-summer. At that time of year the defenders' food supplies are likely to have been fairly low, as much of the previous year's grain would have been eaten while the current year's crops would not yet have been harvested and brought into the castle. The weather was likely to be conducive to siege operations and the besieging army would have a number of months in which to capture a castle before being faced with a long, cold winter outside its walls. The sieges of Bedford and Kenilworth both began in June; those of Dover and Carlisle in July. Although John's siege of Rochester started in late September, this was because possession of the castle was deemed so important that the king felt he had to act the moment he heard that his enemies had seized it. There was no question of waiting until the following year. In any event, he reacted so quickly that Rochester's defenders were given very little time to gather in supplies. A further advantage of starting a siege in the summer was the possibility that a castle's well might run dry. This is exactly what happened during King Stephen's siege of Exeter in the hot summer of 1136. When supplies of water ran out the defenders resorted to drinking wine, cooking with it, baking with it and even using it to put out fires. Inevitably, of course, the wine ran out as well and the defenders were forced to surrender. One cannot help wondering whether they left the castle nursing monstrous hangovers.

The history of medieval siege warfare is full of grim stories of starvation. In his poem *The Siege of Rouen* John Page vividly described the population's suffering during the six-month siege of the city by Henry V in 1419–20.

> *Meat and drink and other vittail*
> *In that city began to fail...*
> *Here bread was full nigh gone*
> *And flesh save horse had they none.*
> *They ate dogs, they ate cats;*
> *They ate mice, horse and rats.*
> *For a horse quarter, lean or fat*
> *At a hundred shillings it was at.*
> *A horse's head for half a pound;*
> *A dog for the same money round;*
> *For thirty pennies went a rat*
> *For two nobles went a cat.*
> *For six pennies went a mouse;*
> *They left but few in any house.*

In practice few garrisons would subject themselves to such miseries unless it was in the hope that a relief force was on its way. This was certainly the case with the defenders of Rouen who believed that any day a French or Burgundian army would break the English siege. On one occasion a false report that the Burgundians had arrived on the scene led the city to ring its bells in celebration. Similarly, the reason that the hungry defenders of Rochester Castle clung on to their half of its shattered keep in 1215 must surely lie in their hope that a relief force from London would come to their rescue. More often than not it was the prospect of starvation rather than starvation itself that led a castle or town to surrender. It was certainly not unknown for defenders to eat their horses and many garrisons were prepared to exist on reduced rations for a time. However, if there was no obvious prospect of relief only the most committed or desperate commanders would fight on and defenders' agreements that they would surrender if they were not relieved in a given time must surely have been preceded by a calculation of when their food would run out.

Starvation was not restricted to the besieged. A besieging force might also experience the pangs of hunger, especially when it was operating in enemy territory and a hostile army was in the vicinity. In these circumstances the besiegers could often become besieged themselves. During the Third Crusade the presence of Saladin's army outside their siege lines at Acre made it extremely difficult for the westerners to gather supplies and led to rampant inflation within their camp. Camped outside the city of Beaucaire in 1216 during the Albigensian Crusade, Simon de Montfort's troops were so hungry that one knight is said to have even suggested cannibalism:

the one who fights worst and gives way to fear it makes sense to eat him first.

More often than not, however, the people who suffered most from a siege were members of the local population. Both besiegers and besieged were quite capable of burning their houses, trampling their crops and stealing their live-stock. In 1265 the isolated Royalist garrison at Pevensey Castle had repeatedly plundered the surrounding countryside and in 1266 the Kenilworth rebels launched extensive raids across the Midlands in the weeks before the siege; a year after the siege had ended the nearby priory had still not been paid for the grain taken from it by the royal army. Sometimes the locals lost more than just their property. Roger of Wendover relates that during their invasion of 1174 the Scots slew men, women and children. It is a grim fact that a garrison that was running out of supplies would sometimes expel what were termed its 'useless mouths' – non-combatants such as the young, the old and the sick, who were consuming rations but contributing little to the defence of a place. Their hope was that the besiegers would either feed them or at least let them pass through their lines unmolested. Besiegers, however, were not always prepared to oblige. On more than one occasion they drove the unfortunate refugees back towards the castle they had come from, concluding that if its garrison was not prepared to let them back in – and feed them – the sight of these starving people, some of whom may well have been from their families, would reduce their will to fight on. When Philip Augustus began his siege of Château Gaillard in 1203 the population of the neighbouring town of Petit Andelys took refuge in the castle. These 1,400 unexpected arrivals soon put the garrison's food supplies under severe strain and, after an English attempt to resupply the castle had ended in failure, Roger de Lacy, the garrison commander, took the decision to evict 500 of the non-combatants from the castle. At first the besiegers allowed these and subsequent groups to depart but when Philip Augustus returned from campaigning elsewhere in Normandy he immediately ordered that no more refugees were to be allowed to pass through the French lines. For Philip, these useless mouths could be turned into inadvertent allies who, by consuming the garrison's food supplies, would hasten the surrender of the castle. It was not long before the last 400 non-combatants were evicted from Château Gaillard. As they approached the French lines they were driven back by a hail of missiles. Terrified and confused, they rushed back to the castle gates only to find them firmly shut. Philip's chaplain, William le Breton, described their plight as they struggled to survive on the barren slopes outside the castle with no shelter against the winter weather and little to eat other than a few wild herbs. They fought over a chicken that had flown out of the castle. They hunted down and ate the castle dogs, which had also been ejected by de Lacy. Some even resorted to cannibalism. When Philip finally took pity and ordered the pathetic outcasts to be fed, over half had perished through exposure and starvation. Even then their suffering was not at an end, for many died when their stomachs were unable to cope with their first proper meal in months.

chapter three

Sieges in the north
1173–74

In 1173 Henry II was faced with the biggest crisis of his reign when his sons Henry the Younger, Richard and Geoffrey rebelled against him, supported by his wife, Eleanor, and Louis VII of France. When news of the rebellion reached the king of Scotland, William the Lion, he at once saw an opportunity to achieve his long-held ambition of winning back Northumbria, which had been in Henry's possession since 1157. Northumbria had already changed hands on three occasions since the Norman Conquest. William II had conquered the region at the end of the 12th century but it had been recovered by David I of Scotland in 1139 when he took advantage of the anarchy in England to secure King Stephen's recognition of his son, Henry, as Earl of Northumberland. David also gained control of Carlisle and Cumbria south of the Solway. In 1149, in a bid to secure Scottish support against Stephen, the future Henry II had promised David that all the land north of the Tyne should belong to the kings of Scotland forever. However, in 1157 Henry, now king, met with David's young successor, Malcolm IV, at Chester and demanded the return of the northern counties. William of Newburgh tells how, faced with an English king who was not hampered by civil war, Malcolm gave way – 'prudently considering that it was the English king who had the better of the argument by reason of his much greater power' – and was granted the earldom of Huntingdon in exchange. When Malcolm died in 1165 he was succeeded as king by his brother, William the Lion. William had a personal reason for seeking the return of Northumbria, for he had succeeded to the earldom on the early death of his father in 1152, only to see his brother browbeaten into giving it away to the English.

Resolving to sell his support to the highest bidder, William made overtures to both King Henry and his rebellious sons. The king offered him nothing, but Henry the Younger promised him the northern counties in exchange for his support so William threw in his lot with the rebels and invaded England with an army bolstered by Flemish mercenaries. Jordan Fantosme, a contemporary chronicler who was present during part of the ensuing campaign, writes that William, who seems to have lacked siege engines, had been advised by the Count of Flanders to lay waste to English territory before besieging any castles. The Scottish king appears to have listened to this advice and it may well

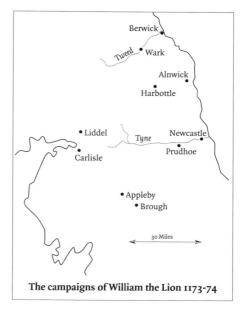

The campaigns of William the Lion 1173-74

be that the ensuing campaign was simply a preparation for a more serious invasion in the following year. Bypassing Newcastle, he marched west along the Tyne, burning and pillaging as he went. According to Roger of Wendover, William

> *marched securely across the territories of the Bishop of Durham, burned several villages, and slaying both men, women, and children, carried off an incalculable booty.*

He soon reached Prudhoe. Set on a massive earthwork at the end of a steep-sided spur above the River Tyne, Prudhoe Castle was an important administrative centre, commanding a fertile stretch of the Tyne valley. At the time it seems to have consisted of two stone enclosures, one entered through a square stone gatehouse, the other housing a small keep. In addition, Prudhoe was of considerable strategic importance. Situated about 10 miles west of Newcastle, it overlooked the main east–west road to Carlisle as well as an important river crossing. It also stood squarely in the path of any Scottish army entering England through the Cheviots at Carter Bar. Despite the advice of the Count of Flanders, William seems seriously to have considered having a crack at Prudhoe.

According to Fantosme,

> *The king of Scotland had his pavilions, his tents, and his marquees pitched there, and his earls and nobles assembled, and he said to his noblemen; 'My lords, what shall we do? As long as Prudhoe stands we shall never have peace'.*

Despite the castle's strategic significance, William's motives in considering an assault were probably as much personal as they were military. Although the castle's owners, the Umfravilles, had been granted the barony of Prudhoe by Henry I of England, the family had enjoyed close connections with the Scottish court, especially when the earldom of Northumberland was in Scottish hands. David had worked hard to win the loyalty of families like the Umfravilles; Odinel d'Umfraville, Prudhoe's owner in 1173, had been brought up in the household of William the Lion's father and the family had been granted land in Lothian and Stirlingshire. As a result, William saw their support for Henry II's reclamation of the northern counties in 1157 as an act of betrayal. In 1173 he probably considered that he had the chance not only to recover Northumbria but also to settle some old scores. In the event, although William's mercenaries were in favour of attacking the castle, the Scottish lords were unhappy at the prospect of a long siege and persuaded their king to carry on westwards towards Carlisle. Prudhoe was left alone – for the time being. With Henry II campaigning in France, affairs in England rested in the hands of Richard de Lucy, Justiciar of England and Umfraville's father-in-law. A veteran of the wars of King Stephen, de Lucy was an energetic soldier. After capturing the rebel town of Leicester and agreeing a truce with the garrison of its castle, he headed north to deal with the Scots. He forced William to retire across the border and launched a retaliatory raid of his own into Lothian, ravaging the countryside before agreeing a truce until the following January in order to deal with the Earl of Leicester, one of the leading rebels, who had landed in England with an army of Flemish mercenaries. That October de Lucy defeated and captured him near Bury St Edmunds. Meanwhile Henry II had enjoyed success across the Channel. As the richest king in Europe, with what William of Newburgh described as 'an abundant hoard of money in the royal treasury', he had been able to hire a large force of mercenary 'Brabanters'. According to the royal clerk, Roger of Howden, they served Henry well ('though not without the large pay which he gave them', he cynically observed), driving Louis back from Verneuil and capturing the rebel Earl of Chester at Dol in Brittany.

Despite these setbacks, the anti-Henry alliance was far from beaten. The following year Louis, William and Henry the Younger joined forces again and in May 1174 William invaded England for a second time. Once again the invasion was accompanied by widespread destruction, looting and – if English chroniclers like Howden are to be believed – murder:

> *Infants, children, youths, aged men, all of both sexes, from the highest to the lowest, they slew alike without mercy or ransom. The priests and clergy they murdered in the very churches upon the altars... wherever the Scots and the Galloway men came, horror and carnage prevailed... Oh, shocking times! then might you have heard the shrieks of women, the cries of the aged, the groans of the dying, and the exclamations of despair of the youthful!*

This time, however, William was after more than just plunder. It is clear that his intention was to wrest control of the region by seizing its castles. Once again the Scots began by laying siege to the motte-and-bailey castle at Wark. Wark was another important frontier castle, commanding a ford across the Tweed. According to accounts from 1174 it had a garrison of 10 knights and 40 squires and had been resupplied to withstand a siege. After his troops had crossed the castle's ditch only to be driven back by the defenders, William brought a catapult, probably a traction trebuchet, into action. It was not a success. According to Fantosme, the first stone it shot 'barely tumbled out of the sling and it knocked one of their own knights to the ground'. Eventually the Scots gave up and headed off westwards; in relief at their departure, Wark's castellan ordered his men not to taunt the departing Scots in case they came back! Leading his army to Carlisle, William summoned Robert de Vaux, its castellan, to surrender, employing a mixture of bribery and threats, offering de Vaux the choice of gold and silver if he handed the castle over or a 'bad death' once Carlisle was captured if he refused. But de Vaux was neither tempted nor intimidated. A loyal supporter of Henry (who had granted his father the barony of Gilsland in order to cement his hold on the region), de Vaux replied that he had no need for gold and silver when he had plenty of wheat and wine, and refused to surrender. Although the region had been thoroughly despoiled by the Scots in 1173 and the population reduced to famine, attempts do seem to have been made by the English to prepare for a second invasion by ensuring that key castles were as well stocked with supplies as they could be in the circumstances. Leaving some of his forces to watch Carlisle, William marched south-east in the direction of Brough. Presumably his intention in doing this was to deny the English the use of what would have been, if all went to plan, an important castle on the southern border of his newly acquired territory. His route first took him past Appleby, a modest castle with a small keep. Fantosme states that Cospatric, Appleby's elderly Saxon constable, put up no resistance at all and surrendered almost immediately. During the English Civil War such a poor showing might well have cost a governor his life, but Henry II took a more pragmatic view of the situation and later fined Cospatric 500 marks instead. William then moved on to Brough Castle. Brough stood on the site of a Roman fort on a steep escarpment above the south bank of Swindale Beck and was one of the first stone castles to be built in England. It was essentially a walled enclosure with a keep at one end, and was defended by six knights and their entourages. The Scots attacked the outer walls in a number of places and, after a hard fight, succeeded in driving the defenders back into the keep. At this point the Scots brought up wood and other combustible material and proceeded to set the keep alight. Despite the fact that the tower was built of stone it must have contained enough wood for the fire to take hold and, as the flames began to spread, the garrison surrendered. One knight, however, remained defiant. He climbed onto the roof, hurled down spears and shouted defiance, until the advancing fire forced him to yield as well.

William then returned to Carlisle where, as Roger of Howden relates:

...he continued the siege, until Robert de Vaux, in consequence of provisions failing him and the other persons there, made a treaty with him on the following terms, namely, that, at the feast of Saint Michael next ensuing [29 September] *he would surrender to him the castle and town of Carlisle, unless, in the meantime, he should obtain succour from his master the king of England.*

Perhaps the previous year's devastation was having an effect. Continuing his campaign to capture strategically important castles, William headed east. He had probably already taken the key border castle of Liddel, a huge earth and timber fortification overlooking a crossing of the river of the same name about 10 miles north of Carlisle. Now he returned to Prudhoe. Fantosme suggests that William was hoping to take the castle by surprise. However d'Umfraville, who had been granted £20 by Henry in order to retain additional knights for its defence, was ready for him:

King William now goes straight to Odinel, intending to take him by
surprise and seize the castle: but the castle was newly provisioned... Odinel
had settled some excellent men in the castle, making it such a fortress that I
never saw better ones anywhere.

According to Fantosme the garrison, knowing that d'Umfraville would have stood little chance of surviving the attentions of the Scots if Prudhoe fell, persuaded him to leave the castle and he reluctantly rode off in search of reinforcements (his departure, of course, removed a major obstacle to their surrendering should the need have arisen). The Scots began by attacking the outer walls of the castle but the garrison stood firm and drove them back. The fact that d'Umfraville later levied labour for the rebuilding of the castle suggests that the Scots had succeeded in inflicting at least some damage upon Prudhoe, but to what extent is not known. Three days later when they heard that a relief force was on its way the Scots abandoned the siege and headed north-east towards Alnwick, but not before they had carried out their customary devastation of the surrounding area:

outside they have lost their fields and their standing crops of wheat and
their gardens were stripped by their evil adversaries; and anyone who
could think of nothing worse to do barked the fruit trees, thus working off
his spite.

The next castle to be attacked was probably Harbottle, a large motte-and-bailey castle on the banks of the Coquet. Facing another invasion route from Scotland, it had been built 15 years earlier by the Umfravilles on the orders of Henry II. Having captured it, William moved on to Alnwick where he divided his army into three, sending two divisions off to ravage the countryside while he blockaded the castle with the third. As events were to show, it was not a wise move.

Meanwhile, further south, the rebel cause was prospering. Earl Ferrers captured Nottingham with the aid of William's brother, David, while Hugh Bigod, another rebel, took Norwich. As a result, on 8 July Henry II, who had been campaigning against his enemies in Normandy, responded to the pleas of his English supporters and returned to England. His first act upon landing was to head straight to Canterbury where, on 12 July, he did lengthy penance at the shrine of Thomas Becket. After walking the last three miles to the cathedral in bare feet, he prostrated himself before the shrine where he was given between three and five (probably symbolic) lashes by each of the clerics present. He then spent the night on the ground in prayer and fasting, surrounded by other pilgrims. A few days later Henry received extraordinary news; on 13 July, the very day after he had completed his penance, William the Lion had been taken prisoner at Alnwick. In Henry's eyes, his prayers had done the trick: God had forgiven him.

Accounts vary as to the precise circumstances surrounding William's capture but it seems the force that assembled for the relief of Prudhoe finally caught up with him. Led by a number of northern barons including Bernard de Baliol and Ranulph de Glanville, and joined by d'Umfraville and de Vesci, the force had mustered at Newcastle before marching by night towards Alnwick. The following morning was misty and the Scots, who had not taken the precaution of sending out scouts to watch for an approaching enemy, initially thought that the force advancing towards them them was part of their own army. When it became clear that they were in fact English William led his knights in a counter-charge but in the ensuing mêlée his horse was killed and rolled on top of him, leaving him with no option but to surrender. Many other leading Scottish nobles surrendered with him rather than be accused of deserting their king. On 26 July, with his legs shackled beneath his horse, William was brought before Henry at Nottingham. The capture of William soon brought the revolt in England to an end. On 7 August Henry crossed the Channel with a large force of Welshmen supplied by his ally, Lord Rhys of Deheubarth, and four days later he relieved Rouen, which had been besieged by the forces of Louis. Support for Henry the Younger rapidly melted away and by September the rebellion was at an end.

Henry was magnanimous to his defeated opponents. His sons were soon brought back into favour, no one was executed or even jailed, and the defeated rebels had their lands restored to them. But William was not treated so generously. He was soon released from captivity by the Treaty of Falaise but only in return for an acknowledgement that his kingdom was a fief held from the king of England. He was also forced to hand over to Henry the castles of Roxburgh, Berwick, Jedburgh, Edinburgh and Stirling and agree to cover the costs of garrisoning them. Although William of Newburgh was to write that Henry now controlled an empire 'from the last bounds of Scotland to the mountains of the Pyrenees', the motives behind these draconian measures were primarily defensive. Henry had won, but William's campaign had shown that the possession of castles alone could not prevent an area from being invaded and ravaged. Furthermore, although he was short of siege equipment, William had still managed to capture at least four English castles in little more than two months. By reducing the Scottish king to the status of a subservient vassal Henry was trying to ensure that the terrible and worrying events of 1173–4 could never happen again.

God on his side? Roger of Wendover's account of the penance of Henry II

He then fasted on bread and water, and would not enter any city, until he had fulfilled the vow which he had made in his mind to pray at the tomb of St Thomas Archbishop of Canterbury and glorious martyr. When he came near Canterbury, he dismounted from his horse, and laying aside all the emblems of royalty, with naked feet, and in the form of a penitent and supplicating pilgrim, arrived at the cathedral on Friday... and like Hezekiah, with tears and sighs, sought the tomb of the glorious martyr, where, prostrate on the floor, and with his hands stretched to heaven, he continued long in prayer. Meanwhile the Bishop of London was commanded to declare, in a sermon addressed to the people, that he had neither commanded nor wished, nor by any device contrived the death of the martyr, which had been perpetrated in consequence of his murderers having misinterpreted the words which the king had hastily pronounced: wherefore he requested absolution from the bishops present, and baring his back, received from three to five lashes from every one of the numerous body of ecclesiastics who were there assembled. The king then resumed his garments, and made costly offerings to the martyr; assigning forty pounds yearly for candles to be burned round his tomb: the remainder of the day and the following night were spent in grief and bitterness of mind. For three days the king took no sustenance, giving himself up to prayer, vigils, and fasting: by which means the favour of the blessed martyr was secured, and, on the very Saturday on which he prayed that indulgence might be shown to him, God delivered into his hands, William king of Scots who was forthwith confined in Richmond Castle. On that same day, also, the ships which the young king his son [Henry the Younger] *had assembled in order to invade England, were dispersed by the weather and almost lost, and the young king was driven back to the coast of France.*

Roger of Wendover's account illustrates the contemporary belief in a God who actively influenced world events. Victory on the battlefield was seen as proof of his approval; defeat as evidence of his displeasure. William of Malmesbury, who saw the Norman Conquest as a judgement by God on a forsaken nation, drew a distinction between the Normans, who spent the night before Hastings in prayer, and the Saxons, who spent it drinking and carousing. As a result, a diligent commander would always seek to obtain the support of God for an enterprise with the result that prayer was seen as an essential part of his preparation. A chaplain was a crucial member of any garrison while an army on campaign would be accompanied by a large number of clerics, the senior the better, whose task was not only to bolster morale by administering spiritual comfort to the troops but also to improve the prospects of victory by enlisting the support of the Almighty. Religion could also be used as a weapon with leaders frequently seeking the excommunication of their enemies, reasoning that they would be less willing to risk their lives if they thought that an afterlife of eternal damnation awaited them. At Hastings William of Normandy underlined what he saw as the moral superiority of his cause by going into battle under the banner given to him by the pope. In 1138 the Archbishop of York turned his attempt to repel the invading Scots into a religious crusade. His victory at Northallerton at the battle of the Standard owes its name to the fact that the English fought beneath a ship's mast bearing a silver pyx and the banners of saints Peter, John of Beverley and Wilfrid of Ripon.

chapter four

Rochester and Dover
1215–17

In 1199 John succeeded his brother Richard as ruler of the extensive Angevin Empire but within five years he had lost Normandy, Anjou and much of Poitou to Philip Augustus of France. As a result he was to spend the next 10 years trying to build up a war chest to finance the reconquest of his lost territories. Although he was undoubtedly successful in this, vastly increasing annual royal income, the arbitrary methods he used in doing so alienated not only weak groups such as townspeople, the Church and the Jews but also, more dangerously, the majority of his barons. Following the failure in 1214 of his military attempt to regain his lost dominions his baronial opponents at home rose against him, demanding a charter of liberties as a safeguard against what they saw as the king's tyrannical behaviour. In May 1215 they seized London and the following month John was forced to agree to their demands, attaching his seal to a document called the Articles of the Barons – the basis of the royal grant later known as Magna Carta. John, however, had no intention of implementing the agreement which, he argued, had been extracted from him by force. When, at the end of the summer, John repudiated the charter with papal support, the barons concluded that as the king could not be restrained he would have to be replaced. Declaring John deposed, they offered the throne to Louis, the eldest son of the king of France.

In September 1215 a party of rebels under the leadership of William d'Albini, Lord of Belvoir, seized Rochester Castle. They were let in by its constable, Reginald de Cornhill, an opponent of John. As the castle controlled the bridge that carried Watling Street across the Medway, its possession would prevent John, then at Dover gathering forces from the continent, from marching on the barons' headquarters in London. John reacted quickly and the rebels in Rochester only had three days in which to gather provisions before the advance guard of the royal army arrived. The garrison is said to have consisted of between 95 and 140 men.

An initial attack on the bridge at Rochester was beaten off but John's forces persisted and on 11 October they entered the city in a surprise attack. After destroying the bridge to hinder any relief force coming from London the royal forces invested the castle, with the king arriving in person on 13 October. John, who despite his reputation could be an energetic soldier when he put his mind to it, set up his camp on Boley Hill to the east of the castle. Mounting five catapults there, he ordered a round-the-clock bombardment, with his men, many of whom were foreign mercenaries, working in shifts to allow the defenders no respite. Roger of Wendover writes that:

> amidst the stones hurled from the petrarias and slings, and the missiles of the crossbowmen and archers, frequent assaults were made by the knights and their followers, so that when some were in a measure fatigued, other fresh ones succeeded them in the assault; and with these changes the besiegers had no rest.

Although a relief force which had set off from London on 26 October failed to get through to them, Roger of Wendover says the defenders still put up a fierce resistance. Hurling 'stone for stone, weapon for weapon' from the castle walls they inflicted heavy casualties on John's forces. Eventually, however, the outer bailey wall was breached. Although a contemporary chronicler from Barnwell Abbey, Cambridge, says that John's siege engines caused the damage, Wendover writes that the collapse of the wall was thanks to the work of miners who had undermined part of the defences. This interpretation may well be correct, because in a writ dated 14 October John had ordered the reeve of Canterbury to oversee the manufacture of as many picks as possible and to send them to him. Furthermore, archaeologists have found what may be a mining trench near the most northerly mural towers on the east side of the castle. With the fall of the bailey the rebels withdrew into the keep. The royal catapults were able to make no impression against its thick walls but John was nothing if not resourceful. Setting his miners to work against the south corner towers of the keep, he sent a writ to his Justiciar, Hubert de Burgh, on 25 November ordering him *to send us with all speed by day and night forty of the fattest pigs of the sort least good for eating to bring fire beneath the tower.*

After John's miners had dug a tunnel under the tower and shored it up with wooden props the cavity was filled with combustible material together with the fat from the pigs and set alight. As the fire took hold, the props supporting the corner tower burned through and its unsupported masonry came crashing to the ground. John's soldiers charged over the rubble and battled their way into the tower, but even now the defenders fought on. The interior of the keep was divided in two by a cross-wall and they retired into the undamaged half and barricaded themselves in, still hoping that a relief force would come to their rescue. But the rebels were running out of supplies. They had already been forced to eat their horses, including their expensive chargers – 'A hard diet for those who were normally used to fine food', as the Barnwell Chronicler commented. Now, in a bid to reduce the mouths they had to feed, they pushed those considered of least military value out of their half of the keep to be seized by John's men, who are said to have cut off the hands and feet of many of their new prisoners. Despite such desperate measures, by 30 November the remaining supplies had been eaten and the defenders were forced to surrender. According to Roger of Wendover, the king was not in a forgiving mood. He writes that John,

on account of the number of his troops slain, as well as the money he had spent on the siege, was greatly enraged, and in his anger ordered all the nobles to be hung on the gibbet.

By the rules of war of the time John was entitled to do this, as he had been forced to storm the castle. However, Savaric de Mauleon, one of his mercenary captains, dissuaded him from this course of action, arguing that it might lead to reprisals and cause his garrisons to surrender for fear of retaliation by the rebels. In the event the captured rebel leaders were imprisoned in Corfe and Nottingham and only one man was hanged, a crossbowman who had previously been in John's service and had deserted. Writing about the siege, the Barnwell Chronicler commented that 'our age has not known a siege so hard pressed nor so strongly resisted' and added that after the fall of Rochester 'few cared to put their trust in castles'. John followed up his victory by heading north to deal with Alexander II of Scotland who had been promised England's northern counties in return for his support for the barons. Rebel lands that lay in the path of John's largely mercenary army were ruthlessly pillaged. According to Roger of Wendover, who admittedly had little time for John:

> the king's enemies wherever they were found were imprisoned in chains and compelled to pay a heavy ransom. Even the priests whilst standing at the very altars, with the cross of the Lord in their hands, clad in their sacred robes, were seized, tortured, robbed and ill-treated... they inflicted similar tortures on knights and others of every condition, some of them they hung up by the middle, some by the feet and legs, some by the hands, and some by the thumbs and arms, and then threw salt mixed with vinegar in the eyes of the wretches, taking no heed that they were made after God's image...others they placed on tripods or gridirons over hot coals, and then bathing their roasted bodies in cold water they thus killed them, and when in their tortures, the wretched creatures uttered pitiable cries and dreadful groans, there was no one to show them pity, and their torturers were satisfied with nothing but their money...

John's fearsome mercenaries soon saw off Alexander and, after recapturing Carlisle and ravaging Lothian, the king and his army returned south. Marching through East Anglia, his forces once again captured the castles and burned the lands of his enemies who by now were spiritually as well as militarily on the back foot, having been excommunicated for their opposition by John's ally, the pope. By the spring of 1216 the rebels were left with little more than London and it must have seemed that John's foreign troops had secured him victory, despite the fact that so many of the major barons of England were ranged against him. But on 21 May 1216 everything changed. Prince Louis landed at Thanet in Kent with a large French army. Roger of Wendover writes that John was at Dover at the time but,

> as he was surrounded with foreign mercenaries and knights from the transmarine provinces, he did not venture to attack Louis on his landing, lest in the battle they might all leave him and go over to the side of Louis; he therefore chose to retreat for a time, rather than to give battle on an uncertainty.

As John retreated to Winchester, Louis recaptured Rochester after a brief siege and then on 2 June, among scenes of great jubilation, entered London. A month later he captured Winchester as well. Alexander of Scotland and Llewelyn of Wales both pledged their support to Louis and a number of those barons who had previously remained loyal to John, including his half-brother, the Earl of Salisbury, chose this moment to desert the king. By late summer, with the help of the French, the rebels had recaptured most of their lost territory. In the south-east only two castles remained loyal to John: Windsor and, crucially, Dover.

Dover was one of the largest and most important castles in the kingdom. Its clifftop site already had a long history of occupation, housing in turn an Iron Age hillfort, a Roman lighthouse and a Saxon burgh, and the Normans had constructed a fortification there shortly after their victory at Hastings. However, the castle of 1216 was relatively new, having been begun by John's father Henry in about 1180, extended by his brother Richard and then further strengthened by John himself. Henry had built a square keep of Kentish ragstone, flint and Caen stone towards the northern end of the hillfort, surrounded by an inner-bailey curtain wall, and had begun the construction of an outer wall which, at the time of Louis' invasion, probably extended southwards and cut across the site a little to the south of the inner bailey. Both bailey walls were generously provided with mural towers from which flanking fire could be directed on attackers. The main entrance to the castle was at the northern end of the site, through a large gatehouse with two drum-towers, almost certainly constructed in John's reign. This gatehouse was protected to the north by a large earth and timber barbican with an oak palisade and wide ditch. The resulting fortress was one of the most up-to-date in Europe with an emphasis on an active, concentric, defence in depth, in which the towers of the curtain walls had greater defensive importance than the keep, which was now as much symbolic and residential as military.

Dover's clifftop location, facing France and overlooking the Straits of Dover, gave it immense strategic importance. It is often said that it 'commanded' the shortest sea crossing between England and the continent although such a statement needs a certain amount of qualification. The limitations of medieval artillery meant that an enemy fleet could sail past the castle with impunity and, on their own, there was little that Dover's garrison could do either to prevent a landing or to stop an enemy army from bypassing the fortress. What made the castle so important to both sides in 1216, however, was its potential as a base for operations. The capture of Dover would have furnished Louis with an ideal supply depot for his campaign of conquest. Not only did it lie at the very end of his supply line back to France but it also had the capacity to house and protect large numbers of men and vast quantities of supplies. On the other hand, if Louis chose to leave the castle alone its garrison would have the opportunity to make a thorough nuisance of themselves, disrupting his communications, intercepting his supplies and ambushing parties of reinforcements for his army. In the event it seems to have been John who best realised Dover's military significance. Although taken by surprise by Louis' landing, he ensured that the castle was well provisioned and furnished with a substantial garrison – contemporary accounts mention 140 knights as well as a great number of men-at-arms – before retreating from Kent. Judging how many men to place in the castle was a fine balancing act. If John sent too few they could be bottled up by a small French force or, worse still, might be unable to defend the castle; if he sent too many he ran the risk of fatally weakening his own field army with the added danger that the over-large garrison might run out of supplies. As it was, John and his military advisers seem to have got the balance just right. Although the garrison was too large to be ignored and was strong enough to mount an effective defence, there is no mention of it suffering from starvation. Furthermore, although it avoided battle with the main French army, John's army was still able to function, marching north to relieve Lincoln which was famously held for the king by Nicola de la Haye.

John also had to decide whom to place in command of the castle. There was no point in filling Dover with men, arms and supplies if its castellan was going to surrender to Louis at the first opportunity. He needed a man with authority and experience but, above all, someone he could trust. Once again he chose wisely, selecting Hubert de Burgh, his Justiciar, for the task. As Justiciar, de Burgh was the man responsible for the government of England, particularly relating to financial and judicial affairs, when the king was out of the country. The younger son of a family of Norfolk gentry, he seems to have entered John's service in the 1190s and made his name by his gallant if ultimately unsuccessful defence of Chinon against the French in 1205. As might be expected of a man who owed his advancement to the king's patronage, de Burgh had remained loyal to John over the years and was to remain loyal to his son after the monarch's death.

When Louis eventually arrived with his army in Dover he spent several days in the town, lodging in the priory. According to an anonymous writer, believed to be a Flemish soldier in the French army, de Burgh often paraded his troops in full armour in front of the barbican where they were shot at by Louis' cross-bowmen. On one occasion a marksman known as Ernaut ventured too near the defenders' lines and was chased down and captured. The siege proper began in mid-July when Louis, after sending his fleet out to sea to complete the encirclement of the castle, divided his forces, keeping some in the town while the rest moved to an encampment on the high ground north-east of the fortress. As a castle Dover had two weaknesses, both of which Louis tried to exploit. The first was that it was built on soft chalk, which was was relatively easy to undermine. The second was that its main entrance was overlooked by the high ground where Louis' troops were camped. It was on this high ground that Louis placed his siege artillery, probably stone-throwing mangonels, which bombarded the outer walls of the castle. He also erected a siege tower, described as 'a very high castle made of wattles'; whether this was a mobile tower intended to be manoeuvred up to the castle or a static one to enable Louis' crossbowmen and archers to shoot over its walls is not clear. Then, using what the Fleming calls a 'covered gallery' to lead up to the wall, Louis' miners dug through the soft chalk and undermined the barbican's timber palisade. Led by Huart de Paon, a knight in the service of the Lord of Bethune, and perhaps supported by missile fire from the siege tower, the French stormed through the breach. The defenders of the barbican, whose commander Pierre de Creon was mortally wounded in the fighting, fell back behind the stone walls.

As the weeks passed by a steady stream of visitors, including Alexander of Scotland, came to the siegeworks to pay homage to Louis. Meanwhile, according to Roger of Wendover, in an attempt to undermine the morale of the garrison, the French

> built a number of shops and other buildings in front of the entrance to the castle, so that the place appeared like a market; for they hoped that they would, by hunger and a protracted siege, force them to surrender, as they could not subdue them by force of arms.

With the barbican in his hands Louis once again set his miners to work, ordering them to undermine one of the towers of the castle's main gate-towers. It seems that the defenders were aware that a new mine was approaching because small tunnels, probably countermines dug in an attempt to intercept the French miners, still exist in the chalk. The defenders may have heard noises, felt vibrations or seen large amounts of chalk soil being carried away, or Louis may have made no attempt to hide what his miners were doing in a bid to undermine the morale of the defenders. In any event, when the mine was sprung and one of the gate-towers collapsed, Louis' men poured forward, only to find that de Burgh was ready for them. After some bitter hand-to-hand fighting the French were driven back. According to the anonymous Fleming:

...a large part of Louis' forces got into the castle, but the people inside drove them out with great vigour, and then closed up the place where their walls had fallen, with great timbers, and crossbeams and palisades of oak trunks.

After the failure of his assault Louis struck a truce with the defenders, but towards the end of October sensational news reached Dover – on the night of 17–18 October John had died of dysentery at Newark, leaving his 9-year-old son Henry as king. Confident that the kingdom was now within his grasp, Louis immediately brought the news to Hubert. Roger of Wendover writes:

Louis then summoned Hubert de Burgh... to a conference, and said to him, 'Your lord King John is dead, and you cannot hold this castle against me for long, as you have no protector; therefore give up the castle, and become faithful to me, and I will enrich you with honours, and you shall have a high post amongst my advisers.' To this offer Hubert is said to have replied, 'Although my lord is dead, he has sons and daughters, who ought to succeed him; and as to surrendering the castle, I will deliberate with my fellow knights.' He then returned to the castle and told his friends what Louis had said, but they were all unanimous in refusing to surrender it to him, lest they might be branded with treachery for a cowardly submission.

Another, more colourfully written, account suggests that Louis tried to persuade de Burgh to surrender through a mixture of bribes and threats, summoning him to a parley at one of the castle's postern gates with four of his supporters. Led by the Earl of Salisbury, Louis' men brought with them de Burgh's brother, Thomas, who had been taken prisoner after Norwich had fallen to the rebels. Accompanied by a bodyguard of five crossbowmen, de Burgh arrived to meet them at the gate and, after his captive brother had begged him to surrender, he was told by Salisbury:

Listen to my advice, Hubert, and obey the will of our lord Louis and he will give you, as an inheritance, the counties of Norfolk and Suffolk, and you will also become his chief counsellor and friend; but if you do not do this, your brother Thomas will be hung and you in a short time will suffer the same punishment.

In this account de Burgh did not waste time conferring with his comrades and instead replied:

Do not speak another word, because by the lance of God, if you open your mouth to say anything more, you shall all be pierced with numbers of arrows, nor will I even spare my own brother.' The earl therefore, and those who were with him, seeing that they would be killed in the flash of an eye because the crossbowmen were ready to discharge their weapons, retreated at once, glad to escape alive and uninjured.

Unwilling to spend any more time bogged down at Dover Louis abandoned the siege and returned to London. He then began campaigning north of the capital. Hertford fell to him on 6 December, followed two weeks later by Berkhampstead. But despite Louis' initial delight at the news of John's death, the event turned out to be something of a blow to his cause for many of the English barons who had joined him had only done so out of personal opposition to what they saw as the tyranny of the late king. They were prepared to overthrow a despot but were less comfortable with denying an innocent boy his rightful inheritance. In November William Marshal, the Regent of England, and Guala, the pope's representative in the country, reissued Magna Carta on behalf of Henry III and many English barons began to waver in their support for Louis. Roger of Wendover records that this was partly caused

by Louis himself, who...in spite of their complaints, had retained in his own possession the lands, possessions and castles of the said barons, which he had subdued with their help and had placed foreign knights and people in charge of them. On the other hand, it seemed a disgrace for them to return their allegiance to a king whom they had renounced, lest they should be like dogs returning to their own vomit; and, being thus in difficulty in every way, they could not mend the broken reed.

Nevertheless, by Easter 1217 three of the country's leading barons – the Earl of Salisbury, the Earl of Arundel and William de Warenne – had deserted Louis for Henry. That April, as hostilities recommenced, Louis began to pay the price for not having reduced Dover, as its garrison, together with guerrillas from the Weald of Kent, began harrying his lines of communication. Anxious to deal with this threat yet unwilling to suspend operations elsewhere, Louis took the fateful decision to divide his forces. On 12 May, with half his army, he once again invested Dover where he constructed a trebuchet, possibly the first to be seen in England and known as *Malvoisin* or *Bad Neighbour*. However, on 20 May the other half of his army was utterly routed at Lincoln by forces loyal to Henry at Lincoln. When Louis received news of this setback he once again abandoned the siege of Dover, fell back to London and sent messengers to France, asking his father for reinforcements. Philip gathered together a sizeable number of troops to help his son, but on 24 August the ships carrying them across the Channel were intercepted off Sandwich by an English fleet under the indefatigable Hubert de Burgh. From their position upwind of the French, the English released lime into the air to blind their enemies before moving in for the kill. Many of the French nobles captured that day were to be imprisoned in Dover Castle. Their commander, Eustace, a former monk and, according to Roger of Wendover, 'a most disgraceful man and a wicked pirate', was found hiding in the hold of his ship, brought up on deck and beheaded. For Louis the naval defeat at Sandwich was the final blow. In September he renounced his claim to the throne and returned to France, having first negotiated good terms for his remaining supporters. Former rebels were absolved from excommunication and, in marked contrast to the aftermath of Simon de Montfort's rebellion 50 years later, were allowed to recover the lands they had held at the start of the war.

Dover Castle had played a significant part in Louis' defeat and had truly been, in the words of Matthew Paris, 'the key to England'. Yet the siege had clearly demonstrated worrying shortcomings in Dover's northern defences and, under a less determined commander than Hubert de Burgh, the castle could well have fallen. As a result, when the war ended a major building programme was undertaken in a bid to eradicate these weaknesses. Initially supervised by de Burgh himself, the work took 40 years. A powerful new gatehouse was built on the west curtain wall, well away from the high ground to the north-east. This new gatehouse was protected from direct assault by the steep slopes to its front; to approach it an attacker would have to advance parallel to the outer curtain wall and be exposed to fire from its battlements and numerous towers. Once the new gatehouse was completed the damaged northern gateway was blocked up for good and two solid towers built over it, next to the surviving tower. A circular tower was built in the moat beyond the old gateway, linked both to a strengthened barbican beyond it and to the main castle by a tunnel that still exists today. Finally the outer curtain wall was completed down to the cliff face and an earth bank constructed around the Saxon church and Roman lighthouse to the south of the castle's inner bailey. By the mid-13th century Dover had become unquestionably one of the most formidable castles in western Europe.

chapter five

Kenilworth 1266

Kenilworth Castle as it is today,
showing alterations made by
John of Gaunt and Robert
Dudley, Earl of Leicester

The arrival of Prince Edward's royal army outside the walls of Kenilworth Castle in June 1266 marked the start of the largest set-piece siege in medieval England. It was also one of the longest and most keenly contested and became a severe drain on the resources of the Crown. The siege was one of the final events in the Barons' Wars of 1264–66 when an alliance of nobles, initially led by Simon de Montfort, challenged the rule of Henry III. On King John's death in 1216 Henry had become king of England at the age of nine and during his minority the government of the country had been in the hands of a number of leading barons. But following his assumption of power in 1227 Henry came to rely on a small number of close advisers, many of them

French, much to the dismay of a substantial number of his barons who saw their power and influence being eroded. Widespread discontent was also caused by expensive failures in foreign policy, while the Church chafed at what it saw as too much papal influence. In 1258 a combination of baronial and ecclesiastical pressure forced Henry to agree to set up a commission for governmental reform. By the Provisions of Oxford of 1259 the commission established a council of 15 members through which the king would govern. The leader of the council was to be Simon de Montfort.

The younger son of Simon de Montfort, the Albigensian crusader and brutal scourge of the Cathars of Languedoc, de Montfort had married Henry's daughter Eleanor in 1238. Created Earl of Leicester in the following year and given custody of Kenilworth castle in 1244, de Montfort was in many ways representative of the French faction favoured by Henry and so despised by the majority of the barons. However, when Henry set aside the terms of the Provisions of Oxford in 1261 and dismissed the ministers appointed by the council, the stage was set for civil war. Dissatisfied with Henry's treatment of some of his family's dynastic claims, de Montfort made common cause with the discontented barons. In May 1264 he led them to victory over the king's army at Lewes and took prisoner both Henry's son, Edward, and his brother, Richard of Cornwall. For a short while de Montfort was virtual ruler of England and, in an attempt to strengthen his position, famously summoned parliaments in June 1264 and January 1265. However, the fragile anti-royal alliance soon crumbled. Support for de Montfort waned and in early 1265 his main rival for the leadership of the baronial opposition, the powerful Gilbert de Clare, Earl of Gloucester, changed sides and declared for Henry.

In May 1265 Henry's son Prince Edward, who had been held prisoner at Kenilworth, escaped from his captors while riding outside Hereford. He is said to have encouraged his guards to entertain him by racing their horses and then, when their mounts were too exhausted to give chase, galloped off to freedom, eventually joining the Earl of Gloucester at Ludlow. De Montfort had also been at Hereford, negotiating with Llewelyn of Wales, but Edward, whose impetuosity had been a key factor in the royal defeat at Lewes, now showed considerable military skill. Raising more troops in Worcestershire, he prevented de Montfort from moving back into central England and reaching his stronghold at Kenilworth. One of de Montfort's sons (another Simon) responded to his father's desperate request for help by abandoning his siege of Pevensey Castle and moving to London. Possibly unaware of the urgency of the situation, he spent three days there, presumably raising troops, before setting off on a rather dilatory journey westwards, which included a lengthy detour in order to plunder Winchester. On 31 July he reached Kenilworth. Believing that Edward and his forces were too far away to be a danger, de Montfort the Younger elected not to keep his troops within the safety of the castle walls. Some are said to have slept in the houses of the adjoining town while others pitched camp in the open. Astonishingly, one chronicler attributes this dangerous course of action to the attractions of the town's baths!

This was why they left the castle: they chose to go out for baths so that, after rising from their beds at daybreak comfortably bathed, they might because of the baths bear themselves more sprucely for battle on the following day, and in the town they could have a great abundance of vessels for bathing than they could well have in a castle...

Reading between the lines, it may well have been that lack of space led to de Montfort's decision not to billet his troops in the castle but, whatever the reasons, the consequences were to be disastrous. That night, showing the urgency that de Montfort seems so obviously to have lacked, Edward made a forced march from Worcester and fell upon the rebel camp at dawn. Taken by surprise, de Montfort's forces were badly cut up and he himself only escaped by swimming across one of the lakes surrounding the castle. Three days later, in an outstanding display of generalship, Edward trapped and destroyed the elder de Montfort's outnumbered troops in a loop of the River Avon at Evesham. Along with his son Henry, and over 30 other knights, de Montfort was hacked to pieces.

This crushing victory led to the restoration to power of Henry III, but the rebel cause was not yet extinguished. Pockets of resistance still remained at Axholme in Lincolnshire and the Isle of Ely – both relatively inaccessible areas surrounded by marshland – and at Kenilworth. In December Edward led an army against Axholme, where de Montfort the Younger had taken refuge, and forced its capitulation. Simon, who seems to have been treated with considerable leniency considering the fate of his father and brother after Evesham, agreed to leave England and surrender Kenilworth in exchange for a pension. However, when de Montfort appeared before the castle and instructed the garrison to hand it over the knights inside refused, declaring that they held Kenilworth not for de Montfort but for Eleanor, his father's widow, who was now in France. Although they knew that they would be spared execution and imprisonment for their parts in the rebellion if they surrendered, their estates had already been pillaged, confiscated and handed out to supporters of the king. Fuelled by the desire to recover their lost lands and the belief that they had nothing left to lose other than their lives, the disinherited rebels in Kenilworth and Ely fought on. De Montfort fled to France.

In March 1266 Henry III again tried to persuade the Kenilworth garrison to surrender peacefully but the defenders gave brutal notice of their intentions when, in a clear breach of the conventions of the time, they returned the king's messenger minus a hand. Their motives for doing this are not clear but it may have been an attempt by the perpetrators to implicate the entire garrison in an act so criminal that it would have been impossible for individuals to slip away and make their peace with the king. Realising that the rebels in Kenilworth were not going to give up without a fight, Henry and his advisors began making plans for a full-scale siege. If the defenders had their motives for fighting on, Henry had his own reasons for ordering what was clearly going to be an extremely costly undertaking. His younger son Edmund's attempts to contain the castle's garrison while the royal army was assembling had been generally unsuccessful and the defenders had launched a number of destructive raids across the Midlands. While Kenilworth remained in enemy hands the surrounding area could never be secure. And the capture of what had been Simon de Montfort's most important castle might well encourage other rebels, notably those in Ely, to end their resistance.

But Kenilworth would not be an easy place to capture. Built on a low hill at the junction of two streams, the castle's defences centred around a massive 12th-century red sandstone keep with a reinforced plinth and corner towers that were virtually solid. In some places its walls were 17ft thick. Surrounding the keep were two strong curtain walls, the outer one added by Henry's father, King John. In addition to stone, Kenilworth was also defended by water. A long, fortified dam held back an enormous shallow lake, known as the Mere, to the south and west of the castle, with a secondary pool to the east. The main entrance to the castle ran along the dam, which was defended by gate towers at each end and by a large semicircular outwork now known as the Brays. The north side of the castle was protected by a ditch. Kenilworth's defences had been further strengthened by the elder de Montfort himself who had ensured that the castle was well stocked with supplies and ammunition and had placed a number of stone-throwing catapults, probably trebuchets, inside its walls.

(De Montfort had learned from an early age just how lethal such catapults could be – in 1218 his father's skull had been crushed by a stone shot from a catapult by the defenders of the besieged city of Toulouse.) Kenilworth was not only strong, it was also well defended. By June as many as 1,200 men had gathered within its walls under the command of Henry de Hastings, a leader of exceptional quality. On 21 June Prince Edward arrived at Kenilworth with the main body of his father's army and began operations at once, setting up catapults – again presumably trebuchets – on the high ground to the north of the castle and to the south across the Mere. Kenilworth's extensive water defences meant that the only realistic way to assault the castle was from the north and it is here that the royal army seems to have concentrated its efforts. As the besiegers' engines began lobbing great stones against the castle the defenders replied in kind. Such was the intensity of the artillery duel that it is said that some missiles actually collided in mid-air. In 1960 archaeologists working in the outer bailey uncovered a number of stone balls that had been catapulted over 300yd from across the Mere and had demolished an outbuilding inside the wall. A number of stones can still be seen in the castle grounds today. In addition to their trebuchets, the royal troops also employed large wooden siege towers designed to enable archers and crossbowmen to shoot down into the castle. However, one of these towers, nicknamed *the Bear*, was brought crashing down by the defenders' catapults. Realising that he and his advisers had underestimated the defenders' capabilities, the king was forced to order up more machines for his siege.

Details of some of the items purchased by the Crown for use during the siege of Kenilworth can be found in the Liberate Rolls of the period (*see* Appendices). Siege engines were obtained from a variety of places: a movable tower was brought from Gloucester; seven engines were built in the Forest of Dean and sent to the siege; two more were sent from Somerset and Dorset to Worcester and then delivered to Kenilworth. Other engines were delivered from London while the gear from one of the king's 'great engines' was sent from Windsor. Other items were manufactured *in situ* with timber from the Forest of Dean, planks from Sandwich and rope from Bridport being delivered for their construction. Because Kenilworth was virtually surrounded by water the besiegers also needed boats. The Sheriff of Worcester is recorded as having supplied a barge while the Sheriff of Gloucester arranged for the delivery of a variety of vessels. It is even said that a number of barges were delivered from Chester and used in an unsuccessful attack across the Mere.

Great numbers of wooden hurdles were needed to provide cover for the soldiers of the besieging army. On 28 July the Sheriff of Oxfordshire was ordered to supply 1,500 and the sheriffs of Worcestershire and Northamptonshire 500 each. Ten weeks later writs were issued to the sheriffs of six counties calling for the delivery of all the hurdles they had. Henry's soldiers also needed ammunition. Vast numbers of crossbow quarrels were used in the siege: 4,000 were sent from St Briavel's Castle in June and a further 6,000 were ordered in July; 30,000 were ordered from Lincolnshire that month while London was ordered to supply another 30,000 in August. Yet, despite all this expenditure, the besiegers do not even seem to have come close to capturing the castle by force of arms. The most they were able to do was keep the defenders bottled up while they tried other means to bring about their surrender.

In July the besiegers resorted to psychological warfare. The Archbishop of Canterbury and two other bishops appeared before the castle walls and solemnly excommunicated the garrison. Some accounts claim that the papal legate Ottobueno (later Pope Adrian V) formally read out the sentence. The purpose of this course of action, which had also been undertaken 40 years earlier at the siege of Bedford, was to lower the morale of the defenders who, it was felt, would be less likely to risk their lives if they believed they faced eternal damnation upon their deaths. But if the besiegers thought this ecclesiastical intervention would lead to wholesale desertions or even surrender they were to be disappointed. Hastings and the garrison made a mockery of the whole affair by dressing up their surgeon in white robes and parading him on the battlements where he in turn 'excommunicated' the king, the bishops and the entire besieging army. Hastings seems to have been an inspiring leader of men and a difficult opponent, and the Royalist who spoke of his 'inordinate pride and violence' was in some ways paying him a backhanded compliment. Although there was some talk of de Montfort the Younger returning to England with an invading army, Hastings knew that, for the foreseeable future at least, he and his men were on their own and realised the importance of maintaining the garrison's morale. To demonstrate the confidence he had in his men and his contempt for the besiegers, it is said that he pointedly left the castle gates open and took every opportunity to mount an active defence, supplementing the fire from his catapults with regular sorties against the enemy positions.

Although the besiegers maintained their military pressure on the castle it was ultimately starvation that offered them the best prospect of forcing its surrender. De Montfort had filled the castle with supplies and the garrison had almost certainly used the time before the arrival of the royal army to stock up on provisions, but there was no prospect of any more food being brought in once the siege began. If the besiegers were able to maintain a close blockade of the castle for long enough the defenders would eventually be defeated – not by catapults and crossbows, but by hunger. However, continuing a full-scale siege for any length of time was an expensive option for Henry and his barons – for both the king's army and his household had to be paid and supplied with food as they sat outside Kenilworth. Any local provisions that had escaped the attentions of the castle garrison were soon used up and surviving financial accounts show that Henry had to cast his net over an extremely wide area in order to obtain the supplies he needed. Food and drink for the royal household could be sourced through the unpopular royal right of 'prise', the compulsory acquisition of provisions (often at rates well below their market value) and the requisition of transport in exchange for bills promising future payment. Large amounts of wine were obtained in this manner from Southampton during the siege and 14 carts were hired by the Sheriff of Oxfordshire and Berkshire to deliver the wine to Kenilworth. Royal forests were scoured for food, with Henry's huntsmen regularly being ordered to provide his household with salted venison. The soldiers of the besieging army were supplied in a variety of ways. Leading magnates who contributed troops as part of their feudal obligations were generally expected to make their own provisioning arrangements while the king could obtain supplies for the troops for which he was directly responsible through the right of 'purveyance', the compulsory cash purchase of victuals in time of emergency. At least 20 counties are known to have supplied food – the Sheriff of London even sent a whale – but the brunt of the effort was born by those counties nearest to the siege. Many bills remained unpaid for some time after the siege and ten Midland counties were so exhausted by their attempts to supply the royal army that they were unable to contribute anything to the exchequer in the following year.

Henry was determined to see the siege through to its conclusion, remaining with his army throughout the whole affair. He knew that it was only a matter of time before he eventually won, but faced with rising costs and a garrison that showed no signs of giving in, he and his advisors decided to moderate their terms of surrender in a bid to bring the siege to an end. In October 1266 they issued the Dictum of Kenilworth, which allowed disinherited rebels to regain their confiscated estates on the payment of fines generally of up to five times the value of their annual income. Although an obvious improvement on total confiscation, these terms were too harsh for the garrison of Kenilworth and the rebels in Ely and both rejected them. On hearing this news Henry resolved to make an all-out effort to capture Kenilworth and summoned a team of masons and labourers to prepare for an assault on the castle walls. By now, however, the defenders were starting to run out of food and to make matters worse disease was beginning to spread through the garrison. Finally, on 14 December, they agreed to surrender under the terms of the Dictum and left the castle unmolested, with their arms, horses and equipment. Hastings eventually joined the Ely rebels who continued to hold out until the following summer when the Earl of Gloucester, who considered the Dictum to be too harsh, occupied London and forced an improvement in its terms.

Immediately after its surrender Henry granted Kenilworth, which despite the efforts of the royal catapults does not seem to have been seriously damaged by the siege, to his younger son, Edmund whom he created Earl of Lancaster. Henry III was to rule England for a further five years. On his death in 1272 he was succeeded by his eldest son who, as Edward I, put into practice in Wales and Scotland many of the lessons he had learned in the campaigns of 1264–66. Henry de Hastings, whose efforts had done so much to improve the terms offered to the disinherited rebels, died in 1268. On 13 March 1271 the Barons' Wars claimed one last victim. Simon de Montfort the Younger and his brother Guy were in central Italy in the service of Charles of Anjou when they learned that Henry of Almain, the eldest son of Richard of Cornwall and the nephew of Henry III, was attending mass in Viterbo. In what seems to have been an unpremeditated act of revenge for the deaths of their father and brother at Evesham the brothers attacked him in church and, despite the fact that Henry had not even been present at the battle, showed him no mercy. 'You had no mercy for my father and brothers' was Guy's reported comment as he stabbed him to death. Simon died later that year in a castle near Siena, but Guy was later arrested for the crime and spent about a year in prison before buying his release and re-entering the service of Charles of Anjou. Captured during an Angevin attack on Sicily in 1287, he died in a Sicilian prison four years later. Henry's murder caused universal outrage and, in his *Inferno*, written 40 years later, Dante placed Guy de Montfort among the murderers in the seventh circle of Hell, submerged to the neck in a river of boiling blood.

chapter six

Alnwick, Bamburgh and Dunstanburgh 1461–64

The popular image of the Wars of the Roses as one long period of bitter dynastic bloodshed is at least in part due to the work of Tudor historians who exaggerated the evils of the period in order to contrast them with the peace and prosperity of their own age. In fact, while campaigns could be nasty and brutish, they were usually very short. According to the Flemish writer Philippe de Comynes, the English were 'of all the people in the world the most inclined to give battle'. He may have been overstating the case when he went on to say that '…if any conflict breaks out in England one or other of the rivals is master within ten days or less', but the fact remains that in over 30 years of so-called warfare there were less than two years of actual campaigning. And because fighting was more about the elimination of rivals than the conquest of territory, sieges of towns or even castles were relatively rare and England was generally spared the scorched-earth tactics employed by its soldiers in the Hundred Years War, when towns and villages were regularly destroyed and large swathes of countryside laid waste. As a result, Comynes could conclude:

> … out of all the countries which I have personally known, England is the one where public affairs are best conducted and regulated with least violence to the people. There neither the countryside nor the people are destroyed, nor are buildings burnt or demolished. Disaster and misfortune fall only on those who make war, the soldiers and the nobles.

The Wars of the Roses were essentially three separate wars, each with different origins. The first was caused by Henry VI's failings as a ruler and the ambitions of Richard of York, who demanded first the lead role in government and then the crown itself. This political tension was exacerbated by a number of bitter family rivalries, such as those between the Nevilles and the Percys, who in part saw the ensuing conflicts as an opportunity to pursue their own agendas. In May 1455 York and the Nevilles attacked the royal court at St Albans and killed a number of leading Lancastrian nobles, but matters did not come to a head until July 1460, when York captured Henry VI at the battle of Northampton and claimed the throne. Though a compromise was reached, with Henry remaining king with York as his heir, Henry's wife Margaret of Anjou refused to countenance the disinheritance of her son, Prince Edward, and raised an army to fight for the Lancastrian cause. York was defeated and killed outside Sandal Castle near Wakefield in December but his son Edward IV's crushing victory at Towton in March 1461 effectively settled the issue. Nevertheless, Lancastrian resistance lingered on in Northumberland for a further three years and Harlech Castle did not surrender until 1468.

The second war, of 1469–71, was primarily caused by the discontent of the mighty Richard Neville, Earl of Warwick. Formerly Edward IV's chief supporter, Warwick saw his influence being eroded following the king's marriage to Elizabeth Woodville and in 1469 he rebelled, capturing Edward after the battle of Edgecote and briefly holding him prisoner until he was forced by popular opinion to release him. In 1470, after the failure of a second rebellion, he made an extraordinary alliance of convenience with his old enemy Margaret of Anjou, forcing Edward into exile and temporarily restoring Henry VI to the throne. However, in 1471 Edward returned to England and brought his enemies to battle separately, defeating Warwick at Barnet and Margaret and her son Prince Edward at Tewkesbury; Henry was murdered the same year. Having disposed of both Henry VI and his son, Edward then ruled virtually unchallenged until his death in 1483, at the age of just 41.

The final phase of fighting was triggered in 1483 by the usurpation of the throne by Edward's brother, Richard of Gloucester. This action fatally split the Yorkist establishment and enabled Henry Tudor, a relatively unknown Lancastrian exile, to emerge as the champion of both York and Lancaster – a position he strengthened by promising to marry Edward IV's daughter, Elizabeth. Later that year Richard defeated a rebellion by many of Edward IV's former servants, led by his own former ally the Duke of Buckingham. Richard had already alienated much of the political nation by favouring men from his power bloc in the north, and grants of rebel land and property to his supporters

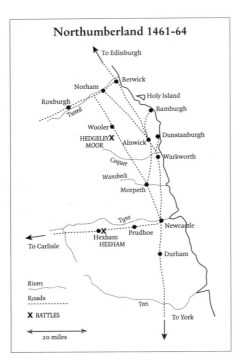

Northumberland 1461-64

To Edinburgh
Berwick
Norham
Roxburgh
Holy Island
Tweed
Bamburgh
Wooler
HEDGELEY **X**
MOOR
Alnwick
Dunstanburgh
Coquet
Warkworth
Wansbeck
Morpeth
Tyne
Newcastle
X
Hexham
Prudhoe
HEXHAM
To Carlisle
Durham

Rivers
Roads
X BATTLES
20 miles
Tees
To York

added to the unpopularity of his regime, at least in the south of the country. So when Henry Tudor launched his bid for the throne in August 1485, although few nobles were prepared to risk life and property by actually joining the rebellion, Richard found it difficult to mobilise support; at Bosworth on 22 August, Richard confronted Henry with what was in reality a much larger army, only to find that some of his key commanders refused to fight for him, preferring instead to see which way the battle went before committing themselves. Richard was killed and Henry seized the throne, successfully defending it against a Yorkist rising at Stoke two years later.

War in the north

One part of England that bucked the general trend of pitched battles over sieges was the far north. After Edward's victory at Towton in 1461 the Scottish borders became, both politically and militarily, an extremely sensitive area. The deep-rooted influence of Lancastrian families like the Cliffords, Rooses, Dacres and, above all, the Percy Earls of Northumberland, together with the proximity of the Scots, meant that rebellion and invasion were always a possibility in this most distant part of the kingdom. In these circumstances it was not enough to win battles; territory had to be controlled and dominated. As a result, along with towns like Carlisle and Berwick, the great castles of the area assumed enormous importance. For the Yorkists places like Alnwick, Bamburgh and Dunstanburgh were bulwarks against the Scots and power bases in a potentially hostile area; for their defeated opponents they were refuges where the flickering embers of Lancastrian resistance could be kept alight. These circumstances ensured that, after Towton, warfare in the area tended to follow the continental pattern where the main objective of a campaign was not to bring an enemy to battle but to win control of his strongholds. The northern campaigns of 1461–64 were primarily fought for the possession of the great northern castles, which changed hands with bewildering regularity. And they were campaigns in which diplomacy, persuasion, bribery and treachery assumed as much importance as military might.

After her defeat at Towton, Margaret of Anjou fled to Scotland with her husband and son and was soon joined by a number of Lancastrian nobles including Lord Roos and the dukes of Somerset and Exeter. Scottish assistance came at a price; on 25 April the vital border town of Berwick was surrendered to the Scots on Margaret's orders. She also promised them Carlisle, the gateway to the western border, but as it was in Yorkist hands it had to be captured first, so a combined force of Lancastrians and Scots laid siege to it. Needing to establish his kingship, Edward had returned south in May, leaving affairs in the north in the hands of the Earl of Warwick and his able brother John Neville, Lord Montagu, who soon proved his worth by relieving Carlisle. In June Lancastrian raiders under Lord Roos reached Brancepeth near Durham where they raised the standard of King Henry VI only to hurry back to the safety of Scotland when Warwick advanced upon them. Further south Edward was faced with the need to suppress outbreaks of popular disorder and a revolt in Wales where Jasper Tudor (the uncle of the future Henry VII) had garrisoned Denbigh, Pembroke and Harlech in Henry's name. Once again, however, Edward had found an able subordinate in Sir William Herbert, who captured Pembroke on 30 September, defeated the Lancastrians outside Caernarfon on 16 October and took Denbigh at the end of January 1462. Only Harlech Castle continued to hold out and, supplied by sea, did so for several years.

Meanwhile Warwick and Montagu were busy reducing the Lancastrian fortresses that had continued to hold out after Towton. The great Percy stronghold of Alnwick yielded to them in September and the coastal castle of Dunstanburgh followed suit the following month, surrendered by Sir Ralph Percy. Warwick garrisoned Alnwick with a hundred of his own men-at-arms but, on Edward's instructions, Percy was allowed to remain as governor of Dunstanburgh. Presumably Edward, mindful of the need to broaden his support in the north, had hoped by this conciliatory gesture to win a Percy over to his cause – but the plan backfired. In November a Lancastrian force under Sir William Tailboys emerged from Scotland and retook Alnwick before marching to Dunstanburgh, where Percy showed his true colours by opening the gates to his old comrades. Meanwhile, further west, a second force of Lancastrian raiders under Sir Humphrey Dacre had seized Naworth near

Carlisle. Concluding that their hold on Northumberland could never be secure while the Lancastrians had a base just across the border, Edward and his advisers decided to use diplomacy in a bid to end Scotland's support for their enemies. Negotiations were hampered by the fact that the regency council that had ruled Scotland since the death of James II was divided into two factions, one of which was sympathetic to the cause of Margaret of Anjou. However, when Margaret left Scotland in a bid to enlist French support for the Lancastrian cause, the Yorkists took advantage of her temporary absence and agreed a truce with the Scots which lasted from June until the end of August 1462, and gave the Yorkists the opportunity to go on the offensive. In July Naworth surrendered to Montagu; Bamburgh was captured by Sir William Tunstall and, after a short siege, Tailboys surrendered Alnwick to a Yorkist force under Lord Hastings, Sir John Howard and Sir Ralph Grey.

In October 1462 Margaret returned from France, having agreed to cede Calais to Louis in exchange for a loan and the services of an expeditionary force of 800 men under Pierre de Brezé, an experienced soldier. After collecting her husband from Scotland, Margaret landed with her army near Bamburgh, which opened its gates to her. The Lancastrians then turned their attentions upon Alnwick. Short of supplies, the castle soon surrendered. Faced with this new challenge, the Yorkists reacted with speed. Only five days after Margaret's landing at Bamburgh, Warwick headed north from London, while the king's ordinance was sent by ship to Newcastle. On 4 November Edward himself was on the march, accompanied, it is said, by 2 dukes, 7 earls, 31 barons and more than 40,000 men – a considerably larger army than that which he had led at Towton. Margaret, who had received little support from the local gentry, knew that her own small army would stand no chance against this massive force. After reinforcing the four garrisons of Dunstanburgh, Bamburgh, Alnwick and Warkworth which, according to one chronicler, she 'victualled and stuffed with Englishmen, Frenchmen, and Scotchmen', she set sail with Henry, Brezé and the rest of her small army for Scotland. But en route, disaster struck. Her fleet ran into a storm and although the royal family and Brezé managed to reach Berwick in a small boat, most of Margaret's soldiers were forced to put ashore at Holy Island where they were soon mopped up by Yorkist forces.

Edward IV had troubles of his own, although of a more personal nature. He reached Durham by mid-November only to be struck down by measles with the result that the Earl of Warwick assumed command of the campaign. Warkworth Castle, which had rapidly surrendered, became the earl's base.

Warwick's plan was to starve Alnwick, Bamburgh and Dunstanburgh into surrender; he had the artillery with which to reduce the castles to rubble but it was essential to capture them with as little destruction as possible if they were then to be used as centres of royal power. Montagu led the besiegers at Bamburgh; the Earl of Worcester and Sir Ralph Grey oversaw operations at Dunstanburgh; while Lord Fauconberg, who had distinguished himself at Towton and had recently been created Earl of Kent, commanded at the blockade of Alnwick. In a letter to his brother John Paston described the proceedings:

My Lord of Warwick rideth daily to all these castles to oversee the sieges. If they need victuals or anything else, he is ready to supply them… I cannot obtain leave to send any of my waged men home. No one can depart – unless, of course, they steal away without permission, but if this were to be detected they would be sharply punished.

As Christmas approached, the beleaguered Lancastrians began to run out of supplies and the defenders of Bamburgh were reduced to eating their horses. What they did not know, however, was that a large Scottish army, under the Earl of Angus and Pierre de Brezé, was marching to their relief. The Yorkists, who were aware of this development and were anxious to bring the sieges to a swift conclusion before the Scots could arrive, offered generous terms to the hungry defenders of Dunstanburgh and Bamburgh, promising to let the men-at-arms inside go free if the castles were surrendered. The Lancastrians soon accepted the offer and by 27 December both castles were in Yorkist hands. Presumably because of his desire to broaden his support, Edward was equally generous towards two of the Lancastrian leaders. The Duke of Somerset, who had led the defence of Bamburgh, had all his lands and titles restored to him and briefly became a favourite at Edward's court. Sir Ralph Percy was allowed to take command of both Bamburgh and Dunstanburgh once he had sworn an oath of allegiance to the new king. The surrender of the two castles left Warwick free to concentrate on the reduction of Alnwick, but on 5 January 1463 the earl received bad news – the Scottish relief force had at last appeared before the castle. Warwick, who was a superb military organiser and administrator but never the boldest of soldiers, immediately raised the siege and withdrew from his prepared positions around Alnwick. The Scots, expecting to have to fight their way into the castle, suspected a trap and made no attempt to engage Warwick's army. During the ensuing stand-off the defenders of

Alnwick took the opportunity to march out of the castle and join their Scottish allies who, having rescued the garrison, withdrew across the border. The next day Warwick's troops entered Alnwick. Many contemporaries believed that the Scots had missed an opportunity to destroy Warwick's forces. The *Warkworth Chronicle* says that if the Scots

> ... *had come on boldly, they might have taken and distressed all the lords and commoners, for they had lain there so long in the field, and were grieved with cold and rain that they had no courage to fight...*'

With the key castles now in his hands Edward returned south, to be followed a month later by Warwick. However, if they thought that they had finally solved the problem of the north they had reckoned without the indefatigable Margaret of Anjou. In March 1463 she once again crossed the border and Sir Ralph Percy, rediscovering his Lancastrian roots for a second time, handed both Bamburgh and Dunstanburgh over to her. Perhaps Edward had been rather optimistic in his hope that Percy would remain loyal to him. After all, the Yorkists had slain Percy's father at St Albans and his brothers at Northampton and Towton. But what happened next was even more unexpected. After the capture of Alnwick Edward had appointed Sir John Astley, a highly regarded knight from Leicestershire, as its captain, with Sir Ralph Grey from nearby Chillingham being given the junior position of constable. Despite having fought on the Lancastrian side at Towton, Grey had served Edward loyally in recent campaigns and he may well have considered that this appointment was insufficient reward for his service. In any event, as a Lancastrian force under Lord Hungerford approached Alnwick, Grey tricked Astley into opening the castle gates to them. Astley was packed off to Scotland as a prisoner and once again the Yorkists were faced with having to subdue Northumberland.

Warwick and Montagu headed north to deal with this new Lancastrian threat only to discover that they were faced with an even more worrying situation. In June 1463, encouraged by more promises by Margaret of Anjou (it was rumoured that she had offered them vast tracts of land in the north and the archbishopric of Canterbury to Bishop Kennedy), the Scots brought their artillery across the Tweed and laid siege to the key border fortress of Norham. The Yorkists were desperate to hold onto the castle – losing it to the Scots would not only have been a strategic setback but also a serious blow to the prestige of Edward's regime, a blow that would have strengthened the hand of the pro-Lancastrian faction in Scotland and possibly encouraged further opposition in England. It was a tricky situation for the Yorkists, with the Lancastrian garrisons of Alnwick, Bamburgh and Dunstanburgh ideally placed to menace the supply lines of any relief force heading north. Yet Warwick and Montagu managed to reach Norham without being detected and, taken by surprise, the Scots panicked and streamed back across the Tweed leaving the border completely undefended. The two Nevilles took the opportunity to launch a destructive incursion of their own into Scotland, burning and pillaging almost at will. Describing the episode in a letter to a Burgundian noble, Edward's great supporter, William Hastings, wrote of the Scots that:

... until the day of judgement they will repent of the favour and help that they gave to Henry and Margaret... I hope that it will leave such an effect and impression as to make them remember for ever the desolation and misery of the Scots nation through God's grace.

The Norham fiasco had been a crushing setback for the Lancastrian cause. It now became clear to even the most pro-Lancastrian Scots that cooperation with Margaret was more trouble than it was worth. To make matters worse, Scotland's traditional ally, France, agreed a one-year truce with Edward in October. Dangerously isolated, the Scots were forced to open negotiations with England. In December 1463 Bishop Kennedy's envoys met with Edward at York and also agreed a truce that was to last until the following October, while talks aimed at achieving a more lasting peace were to be held the following year. Margaret had already left Scotland for France in a vain attempt to retain support from her country of birth and Henry VI was ejected from Scotland and moved to Bamburgh.

Henry and his few remaining supporters were now on their own but in early 1464 civil unrest in other parts of the country and a shortage of funds distracted Edward from affairs in the north and allowed the Lancastrians to enjoy a brief swansong. Despite having been treated as a best friend by the king, the Duke of Somerset deserted Edward and made his way to Bamburgh. He was joined there by Sir Henry Bellingham and Sir Humphrey Neville, two other former Lancastrians who had also been shown favour by Edward. Together with Sir Ralph Percy they mounted a small but effective campaign, capturing a number of important border towns and even seizing Norham, while further west the Cliffords had already retaken their family castle at Skipton. However, on the battlefield they were no match for the Yorkists.

In mid-April Montagu was ordered to make his way north to meet the Scottish delegates and escort them back to York where talks were being held. The Yorkist leader, by now accompanied by about 5,000 men, was confronted by the main Lancastrian army at Hedgeley Moor near Wooler on 25 April. All the usual suspects were there – Somerset, Roos, Hungerford, Grey and Percy – but in the event only Percy's troops put up a fight. The rest melted away and, hopelessly outnumbered, Percy and most of his men were slain.

Meanwhile Edward had at last taken action. Having announced that he would personally lead an army north to deal with the Lancastrians, he gave orders that his siege artillery – including the great guns *London, Newcastle, Dijon, Edward* and *Richard Bombardel* – be prepared. Desperate to win a quick victory before they were crushed by the massive force that Edward was assembling, the Lancastrians advanced south into Tynedale taking Henry VI with them. Their target was, once again, Montagu, but the Yorkist general was too quick for them. Gathering together as many men as he could, he attacked the Lancastrians at their riverside camp near Hexham on 15 May. Somerset's men barely had time to form a line of battle before they were swept away. The defeated Lancastrian leaders were soon to discover that the Nevilles were a lot less forgiving than their king. Somerset, who had been captured during the rout, was brought before Montagu and summarily executed. Roos and Hungerford were beheaded two days later in Newcastle and in the ensuing weeks nearly 30 other Lancastrians suffered the same fate. Humphrey Neville and Ralph Grey were the only Lancastrian leaders to escape, to the relative safety of Bamburgh Castle. Henry VI narrowly avoided being taken prisoner and spent 12 months on the run before being captured in a wood near Clitheroe.

On 27 May Montagu received a substantial reward for his services when he was formally created Earl of Northumberland. The castles of Alnwick, Bamburgh and Dunstanburgh were still in Lancastrian hands but faced with Edward's mighty siege train, with no field army to relieve them and with no prospect of help from Scotland, their fate was effectively sealed. Montagu and Warwick, however, who had been persuaded to remain in the north to assist his brother, were anxious to capture them undamaged.

Warwick and Montagu soon retook Alnwick and Dunstanburgh by the simple expedient of offering their disheartened defenders a free pardon. Alnwick capitulated on 23 June and on the following day Dunstanburgh followed suit. Moving on to Bamburgh, Warwick's herald once again offered a pardon to the garrison, this time however, with the pointed exception of their commanders Grey and Neville, whose acts of betrayal in 1463 had made them marked men. However, Grey and Neville would have been under no illusions about what their fate would be if they fell into Warwick's hands, and by excluding them from the pardon he ensured that they had nothing to lose by fighting on. Warwick had the power to blast his way into the castle but he made a last attempt to avoid damaging its walls, sending his herald to tell Grey that:

> *if ye deliver not this jewel* [Bamburgh], *the which the King, our most dread sovereign lord, hath so greatly in favour, seeing it marcheth so nigh his ancient enemies of Scotland, he specially desireth to have it unbroken with ordinance, if ye suffer any great gun [to be] laid unto the wall and be shot, and prejudice the wall, it shall cost you the chieftan's head, and so proceeding for every gun shot to the least head of any person within the said place.*

By threatening to execute members of the garrison Warwick was no doubt hoping to drive a wedge between the renegade leaders and their soldiers. But Grey was unmoved and his garrison, perhaps unaware of the contents of the herald's latest communiqué, fought on. Reluctantly Warwick ordered his gunners to open fire. Bamburgh was a powerful fortress but its stone walls were no match for the earl's artillery and they were soon breached. A contemporary account describes how *Newcastle* and *London*, two of the king's iron guns, so battered the castle 'that stones of the walls fell into the sea' while *Dijon*, a bronze gun, 'smote throughout Sir Ralph Grey's chamber oftentimes'. As Warwick's men-at-arms and archers moved in for the kill Humphrey Neville, who had taken over command of the castle when Grey was badly injured by a piece of falling masonry, hurriedly negotiated a ceasefire. In exchange for a pardon Neville opened the castle gates and Warwick's men moved in. The injured Grey was taken to Doncaster, tried for treason before John Tiptoft, Earl of Worcester and Constable of England, and found guilty. Passing sentence, Tiptoft told Grey that he deserved to be 'degraded' by having his coat of arms reversed and his spurs hacked off by the master cook, who was 'ready to do his office with apron and knife' but that the king had decided to spare him this disgrace because their grandfathers (Richard of Cambridge and Sir Thomas Grey) had been executed together at Southampton in 1415. How much of a consolation this was to Sir Ralph as he was drawn to the scaffold on a hurdle and then beheaded is open to debate.

chapter seven

Norham 1513

Although James IV of Scotland had previously supported the Yorkist pretender Perkin Warbeck against Henry VII, in 1502 he agreed a treaty of 'perpetual peace' with England and in the following year married Henry's daughter, Margaret. One of the clauses of the treaty, which was underwritten by the Papacy, was that if either ruler flouted its terms he would be excommunicated. In these circumstances it was perhaps inevitable that the defensive alliance that James concluded with Louis XII of France in 1512 would lead to trouble. When Henry VIII invaded France in the following year, Louis asked James, whom he had been supplying with money and arms, to support him by invading England, and the Scottish king duly obliged. Henry had been expecting such an attack. He knew that Louis had been equipping the Scots and, as the Tudor historian Edward Hall rather charmingly put it:

> *he and his council forgot not the old pranks of the Scots which is ever to invade England when the king is out...'*

As a precaution, Henry only took troops from the south and Midlands to France and left his northern levies under the command of Thomas Howard, Earl of Surrey, his lieutenant-general in the north. On 17 August James's Scottish army headed south out of Edinburgh and five days later it forded the Tweed at Coldstream. The 40,000 men that James led into England were probably the largest and best-equipped force ever to leave Scotland. Many of James's soldiers had recently been armed with pikes, 16ft-long spears which, as the Swiss had proved on numerous occasions, could be a devastating weapon in the hands of disciplined, well-trained soldiers. The fact that most of his men were completely unused to their new weapons does not seem to have bothered James.

The artillery train that accompanied James's army was one of the finest in Europe and was the result of a century of development. The Scots seem to have been using guns since the 1380s and by the 15th century were manufacturing their own small iron pieces, though their larger guns were imported from overseas, in particular from the Low Countries. James II of Scotland was especially interested in artillery; in 1457 the delighted monarch received an enormous iron bombard as a gift from Phillip III of Burgundy. Later dubbed *Mons Meg*, this 8-ton behemoth was capable of firing a 400lb stone ball to a distance of nearly 2 miles. Her huge size made her unwieldy – she is believed to have needed more than a hundred men to handle her and could be moved little more than three miles a day – and she was taken out of service in the 16th century and retired to Edinburgh Castle where she was used to fire salutes at important state occasions. In 1558 she was fired to celebrate the marriage of Mary Queen of Scots to Francis, the French Dauphin; the stone was found nearly two miles away. *Mons Meg* was last fired in 1681, in a salute to the Duke of York that burst her barrel. After spending the second half of the 18th century in the Tower of London she was returned to Edinburgh in 1829 and can still be seen in the castle today.

James II's fascination with artillery was to end in tragedy. He was standing near a cannon at the siege of Roxburgh Castle in 1460 when it blew up, fatally injuring him. His successor, James III, seems to have obtained the first bronze guns from France in the 1480s. More accurate than their iron counter-parts, these could take a larger charge of gunpowder and were able to fire iron balls which were far more destructive than stone ones. Bronze guns were also lighter and easier to transport. James IV continued to acquire artillery and also developed the Scottish gunfounding industry, bringing French experts over to Scotland in 1505 and appointing a Midlothian man, Robert Borthwick, as his 'master meltar' in 1509. James took 17 large guns into England with his army. His train of artillery included five bronze cannon, each capable of firing a 60lb shot, and two 20-pounder culverins. These were probably cast by Borthwick in Edinburgh Castle and were known as James's 'seven sisters'. Moving these guns was a major logistical task: a single cannon needed 36 oxen to pull it along, attended by 9 drivers and 20 pioneers to clear the way.

The Scottish army's primary objective as it crossed the Tweed was the Bishop of Durham's border fortress at Norham. Because the diocese of Durham was so far from London its bishop was given a wide range of devolved powers and duties to enable the king's government to function there on a day-to-day basis. One of the bishop's duties was the defence of the border with Scotland and to that end he was given both the power to raise troops and the possession of the vital fortress of Norham. To differentiate his ecclesiastical and civil functions, the Bishop of Durham used two seals – the almond-shaped seal of a cleric and the oval seal of a nobleman – while the arms of the diocese were set against a crosier and a sword instead of the usual two crosiers.

Described by Sir Walter Scott as 'the most dangerous place in England', Norham overlooked one of the best fords across the Tweed and therefore commanded a major invasion route. As a result it had seen plenty of military action through the centuries. Stormed by the Scots on three occasions, in 1136, 1138 and 1322, Norham had successfully resisted them on six others – in 1215, 1318, 1319, 1327, 1463 and 1497, when James IV's army had dragged *Mons Meg* all the way from Edinburgh in an attempt to batter the castle into submission. Norham occupies a strong defensive position, built on the site of what may well have been an Iron Age hillfort and protected by a ravine to the east and by the steep banks of the Tweed to the north and west. Dating from the 12th century, the castle consisted of a large red sandstone keep within an inner bailey, which in turn was enclosed by an outer bailey with gates on the south and west sides. A third bailey, to the south-east, had probably fallen into disuse by the time of the siege.

The castle had sustained serious damage during the siege of 1497 and in the early 16th century Bishop Thomas Ruthal carried out a number of improvements and repairs, including the rebuilding of the castle's west gate. When, in 1513, it became clear that war was inevitable, the Earl of Surrey wrote to John Anislow, the governor of Norham, to tell him that if he thought that the castle was in any danger he would do as he had done in 1497 and march to its relief. But Ruthal had been supplying Norham with weapons, ammunition and supplies since rumours of war began and Anislow was in a confident mood. Replying to the earl he said that he 'prayed God that the king of Scots would come with his puissance' because he would hold Norham for so long that King Henry himself would have time to come back from France and raise the siege, an answer which, according to Hall, 'rejoiced the earl much'. However, both Surrey and Anislow had reckoned without James's powerful siege artillery.

After crossing the Tweed on 22 August (in an operation that went considerably more smoothly than that of 1497, when several of James's wagons had got stuck on the river bed) the Scots invested Norham. Local tradition has it that James initially positioned his guns on the Scottish bank of the Tweed until a traitor from the garrison advised him to move them to the east of the castle. It seems unlikely that James would have needed such advice as he already knew the area, having besieged the castle 16 years earlier, though it has been suggested that he may have bombarded the castle from across the Tweed before fording the river. Where exactly James planted his guns having crossed the Tweed is open to question. He does not seem to have positioned them immediately to the east of the castle, for the wall there is the least damaged part of the medieval fabric. In any case the presence of a ravine to the east of the castle would have made it almost impossible to attack from this direction and therefore pointless to breach the walls in this area. It is more likely that James positioned his guns further south, on a ridge about 440yd from the walls, or further west where they could be brought to bear on the castle's west gate.

Despite appalling weather James's guns made short work of Norham's defences. Within two days they had, as Hall put it, 'sorely abated the walls', bringing the stonework crashing down, damaging the keep and opening up a breach in the walls of the outer bailey. Over the next three days the Scots launched three major assaults, forcing Anislow's men, who were running short of ammunition, back into the inner bailey. On the sixth day Anislow surrendered. Hall recounts the events:

> ...the King of Scots with his great ordinance had razed the walls of the castle of Norham, and had made three great assaults three days together, and the captain valiantly defended him, but he spent vainly so much of his ordinance, bows and arrows and other munitions that at the last he lacked, and so was at the sixth day compelled to yield him simply to the king's mercy. The castle was thought impregnable if it had been well furnished, but the Scots by the indiscreet spending of the captain, took it in five days...

This seems a little harsh on Anislow; once the castle walls were breached he would have been unlikely to have been able to keep an army of 40,000 men at bay without the liberal expenditure of ammunition. Anislow was packed off as a prisoner to Falkland Palace in Fife and the Scots took possession of the castle. Norham had been too badly damaged to garrison and so the Scots contented themselves with thoroughly looting the place and tearing down what remained of its walls and gates, leaving little more than the central keep standing. Ruthal was devastated when he learned of the disaster. In a letter to Thomas Wolsey he wrote that the fall of Norham 'touched me so near with inward sorrow that I had rather to have been out of the world than in it'.

James's triumphant army moved on to capture the castles at Wark, Etal and Ford, all of which surrendered rather than face the might of the Scottish artillery. Yet, less than two weeks later, James was dead. Brought to battle on 9 September by the Earl of Surrey at Branxton near Flodden, his army was destroyed. The Scottish artillery, so devastating in the context of a siege, proved too slow and heavy to be used effectively on a battlefield and were outshot by the lighter and more manoeuvrable English guns. Carrying their unfamiliar pikes, James's infantry lost momentum and cohesion as they struggled across the boggy ground at the foot of Branxton Hill, and Surrey's soldiers cut them to pieces with their tried-and-tested bills. All of the Scottish guns fell into English hands, to be temporarily stored after the battle in the basement of the tower-house at nearby Etal Castle. Almost unnoticed, James had been cut down in the thick of the fighting. Excommunicated by the pope for breaking the terms of the treaty of perpetual peace, he never received a funeral and his remains were bundled off to England, first to Berwick and then to Richmond Palace. Fifty years after his death some workmen found his body, dumped in the back of a storeroom.

Despite their ultimate victory, the fall of Norham had graphically proved to the English that medieval walls were no longer proof against modern siege artillery. Once Norham was recovered a major rebuilding programme was undertaken, not only to improve the durability of the castle but also to enable it to mount guns of its own more effectively. An artillery bulwark, known as Clapham's Tower, was added to the south inner bailey wall and the roof of the keep was strengthened to enable it to support cannon. By 1521 Thomas Dacre, deputy captain of the castle, felt able to write of the inner ward that 'with the help of God and the prayer of St Cuthbert it is impregnable'. The outer bailey wall was also reconstructed, part of its rampart was heightened, a casemate battery was constructed on the north-west side of the castle overlooking the Tweed, and by 1523 the round towers on the south side of the wall had been replaced by angled bastions designed to provide a wider field of fire. In that year the Earl of Surrey was reported to have constructed 'diverse platforms, ramparts and [mended] broken places with turves and walls of earth'. This may refer to the ongoing strengthening of the outer bailey, but archaeological investigations by English Heritage have also shown that the west gate of the castle, which was not covered by the new artillery towers of the outer bailey wall, was given extra protection by what seems to have been the rather hurried construction of a series of angular earthworks. Two of these appear to have been intended to house artillery while two others, built on ground that sloped too much to be suitable for cannon, were probably intended to shelter infantry and enable them to pour flanking fire on anyone approaching the gate. Indeed, with two fords across the Tweed within a mile to the west of the castle, this must have seemed the most likely avenue of approach for an enemy force.

Yet despite all this expenditure Norham does not seem to have been particularly well maintained. In 1542 Sir Robert Bowes reported that the castle was in good condition and 'stuffed with artillery' but nine years later he was more critical, pointing out the weakness of the outer bailey wall and the failings of its towers, which he considered 'were not ingeniously devised'. In 1559, following Bishop Tunstall's refusal to acknowledge Elizabeth I as Head of the Church in England, the castle was seized by the Crown and in 1561 Rowland Johnson, a military engineer, was sent from Berwick to inspect its defences. His report was damning, pointing out faults in the castle's design, noting decay caused by lack of maintenance and recommending that Norham be replaced by a new, purpose-built artillery fort. The once-mighty castle was gradually allowed to fall into ruin and when, in 1603, James VI of Scotland also became James I of England, the military importance of the site finally came to an end.

chapter eight

The impact of gunpowder: siege warfare in the Civil War

Although catapults had been replaced by cannon and crossbows by muskets, many of the techniques of 17th-century siege warfare would have been instantly recognisable to the 13th-century conquerors of Rochester and defenders of Kenilworth. Unless a surprise attack was being attempted, a set-piece siege would normally begin with a formal summons to yield and surrender negotiations would often continue during the siege's progress. Attempts were often made to undermine walls or scale them with ladders and in 1645 the Herefordshire Royalists even constructed a siege tower. Finally a besieging army that was unable to take a castle by storm would frequently sit down before its walls and attempt to starve the defenders into submission.

By the time of the Civil War, however, there were some important differences in siege techniques, mainly brought about by the introduction of gunpowder artillery. As the Earl of Warwick had shown when he reluctantly battered Bamburgh into submission in 1464, a medieval castle with its lofty walls and high towers now stood little chance against cannon. It was clear that new types of fortification were needed if these devastating weapons were to be resisted. The solution came from the architects of the Italian Renaissance who constructed strongholds with thick low walls that were not only capable of resisting enemy artillery but also of mounting guns of their own. Angular projections were later developed so that guns mounted on them could sweep all approaches to a fort, leaving no dead ground to shelter an attacker. In the late 1530s when England was threatened with invasion, the forts built to guard the coast against an invading fleet were essentially low gun-platforms, which normally had semicircular bastions around a higher, central tower. However, the last to be built – Yarmouth on the Isle of Wight – was very different. Square in plan with a projecting arrowhead-shaped bastion in one corner, it was a forerunner of the extensive Elizabethan fortifications of Berwick-upon-Tweed which are said to have cost over £100,000.

Meanwhile the Dutch were developing a much cheaper form of defence. Often lacking the time and resources to build in stone, they constructed their bastioned fortifications in earth. A banked-up wall of earth was quick to build, relatively easy to repair and as resistant to cannon fire as masonry. And once it was protected by a timber palisade it was equally hard to climb. Such ideas spread rapidly with the result that in civil war England, where defences often had to be put up in a hurry and there were few 'modern' fortifications away from the coast, some places relied entirely on earthworks for protection. Garrisons of the many medieval castles that were pressed into service in the Civil War often built earthworks to keep the enemy at a distance, to accommodate larger garrisons or simply because they had little faith in their old walls. In September 1643, for example, Colonel John Boys surrounded Donnington Castle near Newbury with large earth bastions, the remains of which can still be seen today. Even if a garrison was unable to dig earthworks around a castle it often tried to at least reinforce its walls by piling earth against them.

Clearly no two sieges were alike and the way in which they were conducted was influenced by a number of factors – the nature of the ground, the type of fortress being attacked, the character of the commanders and the urgency of the military situation. Nevertheless, formal sieges often followed a fairly predictable pattern. A besieging army would begin proceedings by digging trenches around a fortress, known as lines of circumvallation, to contain its garrison and prevent supplies and reinforcements from getting through to them. Similar trenches could also be dug to protect the besiegers from attack by a relieving army. These lines of circumvallation could be quite extensive, especially where they incorporated earthwork fortifications or buildings that had not been destroyed by the garrison. Those dug by the Parliamentarians at Newark stretched for over 13 miles. While these lines were being dug the besieging army's gunners would position their artillery, after first examining the enemy's defences to establish the best place to direct their fire. Guns and gunners were often protected by a screen of large wicker baskets, known as gabions, which were filled with earth. The guns themselves would be mounted on wooden platforms to prevent them from being driven into the ground when they recoiled. A huge variety of guns of different calibre were used during the Civil War, which must have made keeping them supplied with the right ammunition a logistical nightmare. Information about the various types of artillery of the period is contained in a number of contemporary manuals although, almost inevitably, they fail to agree in their details.

The following is drawn from Ward's *Animadversions of Warre*, published in 1639.

Name	Weight of shot	Point-blank range (paces)	Maximum range (paces)	Men/horses to draw it
Cannon of 8	64lbs	300	1500	90/16
Demi-cannon ordinary	32lbs	350	1700	60/10
Culverin	16¼lbs	420	2100	50/8
Demi-Culverin	11¾lbs	380	1800	36/7
Saker ordinary	5¼lbs	300	1500	24/5

The besieging gunners might also use mortars to lob great stones or explosive shells, known as granadoes, from a high trajectory into castles or towns. The effects of this could be psychological as well as physical; at Lathom House it was said that even 'the stoutest soldiers had no heart for granadoes'. At Goodrich, however, although Birch's mortar caused extensive damage to the castle, it seems to have had no effect whatsoever upon the morale of the hard-bitten defenders. Firing a granadoe could be an extremely dangerous task, as both the fuse of the mortar and that of the shell had to be lit. If the mortar failed to fire the bomb would explode, with disastrous consequences for both mortar and crew.

Although the largest gun in Ward's list, the cannon, would make short work of most castle walls, such guns were relatively few and far between and extremely difficult to transport. As a result small local garrisons were usually spared their attentions. In fact it also seems that castle walls could be remarkably resilient, even against some of the larger guns. Walter Erle deployed a demi-cannon against Corfe in 1643 but although it was fired at virtually point-blank range it appears to have caused minimal damage to the castle. Of course this may have been as much due to the deficiencies of the crew as the strength of the walls, as trained gunners were in short supply, especially in the early stages of the war. One (admittedly Parliamentarian) account of the Royalist attack on Blackburn at Christmas 1642, for example, claims that the only damage that a demi-culverin managed to cause in 24 hours' non-stop bombardment was to the bottom of a frying pan.

While their guns battered the enemy defences the besiegers would dig zigzag trenches, known as saps, towards the fortification to enable it to be approached in some degree of safety. The primary objective of such a bombardment was to cause a breach in the defences wide enough to be assaulted. However, if their artillery was not powerful enough to do this the besiegers might, like their medieval predecessors, try another tactic and send men forward to undermine the walls. When the saps had been dug and the fortress walls weakened or undermined it was again customary for the besiegers to send a drummer or trumpeter forward with a final summons to surrender. If the summons was accepted, both sides would appoint commissioners to discuss terms. However, if it was rejected or the two sides were unable to come to an agreement, things could get messy. The besiegers would bring down the wall, either by a final concentrated burst of gunfire or by exploding their mine, and their assault troops would leap out of the trenches where they had been sheltering and rush forward to assault the breach, often under heavy fire. It was the custom of the time that defenders who forced besiegers to storm a fortress or town were not entitled to quarter if it fell. Indeed, men who had seen their comrades shot down as they ran towards the breach would not necessarily be in the mood to offer it anyway. One Royalist officer who was present at the storming of Bristol in July 1643 later wrote:

twould grieve one's heart to see men drop like ripe fruit in a strong wind and never see their enemy.

Not all sieges followed this pattern. Sometimes, as at Pendennis in 1646, the besiegers made no attempt to storm a fortification and were content to sit outside and starve the defenders into surrender. On other occasions, for example at Beeston in 1645, the objective of the besiegers was less to capture the castle than to prevent its garrison from causing mischief elsewhere. On the other hand some commanders were in more of a hurry. Some wanted to capture a fortress before an enemy force could come to its rescue. Other leaders preferred to risk losing a few men in an assault rather than see their army reduced by the desertion and sickness that inevitably accompanied a long siege. Others believed that a direct attack offered the best chance of capturing a castle. In 1643 the Parliamentarians tried unsuccessfully to take Corfe Castle by escalade – climbing up ladders that they placed against the castle walls. The previous year Sir William Waller, despite having no siege artillery, succeeded in capturing Farnham Castle by getting one of his soldiers to blow in its gates with a petard, a metal pot filled with explosive that had to be fixed manually to a gate or wall. Even if the petardier managed to reach the gate without being shot by the defenders, he still risked being 'hoist with his own petard' when the device actually exploded. In his *History of Myddle*, Richard Gough relates how one George Cranage had to be 'well lined with sack' before using a petard to blow down the door of Oswestry Castle. Writing to Parliament in November 1643 Waller describes another attempt to use a petard, this time at the Marquess of Winchester's Hampshire stronghold of Basing House:

> *...our men gained the rampart, and the petardier applied his petard, but unluckily mistook the place – for whereas he should have applied it to a place in the old wall which was but a brick and a half thick, he set it against a door that was bricked up and lined with earth, so that it took no effect.*

Sometimes commanders replaced the slow and steady approach of the formal siege with the rapid application of overwhelming force. This was the tactic used in the months after their victory at Naseby by Thomas Fairfax and Oliver Cromwell. Equipped with a powerful siege train that included two demi-cannons and a mighty 64-pounder cannon royal, they mopped up a series of Royalist garrisons in the south-west. On 23 July Bridgwater was stormed. On 15 August Fairfax's troops stormed Sherborne Castle after his great guns had battered a breach in its wall wide enough for his men to march through 10 abreast. Bristol was stormed in September, as was Berkeley Castle. In October it was the turn of Basing House. Two previous sieges of the great old house had been failures, as had an attempt to starve the defenders into submission. Colonel John Dalbier had already begun the bombardment of the house and the works surrounding it when Cromwell arrived with the siege train at Basing on 8 October. Despite Cromwell's warning that he could expect no quarter if he forced the Parliamentarians to storm the place, the Marquess of Winchester refused to surrender. On 12 October Cromwell ordered his guns to open fire. Within a day two large breaches had been opened in the walls and at 6.00am on 14 October five regiments of the New Model Army hurled themselves at the breaches with a ferocity fuelled by the knowledge that the garrison were all Catholics. The outnumbered defenders were swamped. A Parliamentarian soldier describes part of the final assault:

> *...at daybreak we began the storm; and our soldiers, with undaunted courage, got over the enemy's works, entered the breaches, and possessed part of the new house, and the court, betwixt that and the old house, where the enemy had lain a trail of powder, which they blew up...then they in the house threw hand granadoes out of the house, at our men, into the court; but we made our passage into the house amongst them, and by force of arms, appeased their rage...*

As the Parliamentarians rampaged through the burning house 74 of its defenders were put to the sword, including one woman. According to Hugh Peters, chaplain to Parliament's Train of Artillery 'her railing provoked our soldiers (then in heat) into a further passion'.

According to the historian Charles Carlton, out of the 645 military actions he has identified in the three civil wars, 198 were sieges. The places besieged ranged from towns and cities of major strategic and economic significance to smaller garrisons with a more local importance. Many of the latter were housed in castles or fortified houses, often built centuries before the introduction of gunpowder. Indeed, it is ironic that many of Britain's medieval castles saw their most sustained military action in the 17th century, a time when they were technically obsolete. Of the five civil war sieges discussed at length in this book, four of the castles involved – Beeston, Corfe, Goodrich and Wardour – were essentially medieval buildings. Only Pendennis, with its low, round walls and angular bastions and ramparts, had been built in the age of artillery. Even then its original purpose had been to mount guns to protect the Fal estuary from a seaborne attack, not to withstand a land-based siege.

Wardour, Corfe and Goodrich were essentially local garrisons, seeking to maintain some degree of control over the surrounding area or to at least to make life difficult for the opposition. Garrisons such as these would normally be allocated, or often simply take control of, an area which they would 'protect' in exchange for regular payments by its inhabitants. Whether the local population actually wanted this protection is open to question, although the propagandists on both sides did their bit by portraying the enemy in as uncomplimentary terms as possible. Needless to say, individuals or villages who resisted or failed to pay ran the risk of having their goods seized and their houses burned. Settlements that were unfortunate enough to be situated between two opposing garrisons often had the worst of both worlds as they could find themselves being asked to pay contributions to both sides. In 1644, for example, the Wiltshire hundred of Potterne and Cannings was faced with simultaneous demands for money towards the wages of the garrisons of both Royalist Devizes and Roundhead Malmesbury.

In theory garrisons were supposed to gather money and supplies for the war effort in general, but in practice they frequently spent most of their energy looking after themselves. A field commander would often try to bolster his forces by drawing reinforcements out of friendly garrisons but local commanders could be more than a little reluctant to let them leave. In the summer of 1643 Sir William Waller had to write a stinging letter to Nathaniel Fiennes, the Roundhead governor of Bristol, before he would release part of his garrison to reinforce the local Parliamentarian army. Indeed it is worth bearing in mind that a substantial proportion of civil war soldiers fought no battles at all, and very few skirmishes, and spent most of their time on garrison duty. The Parliamentarian garrison of Great Chalfield near Bath is a good example. Consisting of a troop of horse and two companies of foot – as many as 400 men – their main war service seems to have consisted of keeping an eye on their Royalist counterparts in nearby Lacock.

Other garrisons – Goodrich is a case in point – could be extremely active in their prosecution of the war effort but the fact remains that their very existence reduced the number of men available for service with the main field armies. In June 1645 nearly half the troops that Charles I had under arms were scattered in garrisons throughout the country. A recent study of the north Midlands has identified 30 Royalist garrisons in Shropshire alone, and between the defeat of Charles's outnumbered army at Naseby in June 1645 and the Parliamentarian capture of Harlech in March 1647 no fewer than 81 Royalist garrisons are reported to have surrendered. In some ways it may have suited the king to have many of his soldiers dispersed in this manner as it at least spared him the problem of finding the food to feed them and the money to pay them. Nevertheless it is tempting to speculate over what might have happened had at least some of these troops been with him at Naseby.

chapter nine

Wardour 1643–44

On the face of it, Old Wardour Castle (which takes its name from the fact that a new house was built near to it in the 18th century) seems a highly unlikely location for two civil war sieges. Tucked away in the hills near the Wiltshire village of Tisbury, Wardour's strategic importance was negligible: it controlled no important line of communication and was too small to house a major garrison. Even in medieval times the purpose of the castle had been more residential than military, with walls overlooked by high ground on three sides and battlements built more for show than combat. Sixteenth-century remodelling had further weakened Wardour's somewhat flimsy defences, enlarging the windows to let in more light. A couple of large siege guns would probably have made short work of the castle's 14th-century walls, but in the event the castle's military insignificance worked in its favour: neither Roundheads nor Royalists were prepared to divert such valuable and rare resources for use against such a minor target. So although Wardour came under sustained bombardment on the two occasions that it was besieged, the guns employed by the attackers were never large enough to do any significant damage.

When civil war broke out in England in 1642 Wardour's Catholic owner, Thomas Lord Arundell, joined the Royalist cause. He was serving with the king's army in April 1643 when his castle came under attack by forces under Sir Edward Hungerford, a prominent local Parliamentarian. Because of the castle's limited military importance, Hungerford's actions were primarily an attack on a local political rival and a bid to prevent Arundell's resources being used to support the king. With Arundell absent the defence of the castle was left in the hands of his wife Blanche, with a garrison of little more than 25 men supported by a smattering of household servants, many of whom were women. Sir Edward placed his two guns on the high ground overlooking the castle entrance but although they bombarded the castle for six days, breaking some windows and damaging a fireplace (probably in the great hall), they had little effect on the structure of the castle. According to a Royalist newspaper the Parliamentarians then set off mines in the service tunnel leading to the castle cellars and in a second tunnel draining the latrines. Although both explosions seem to have done little harm or damage, they were enough to cause the garrison to surrender on 8 May 1643. Edmund Ludlow, Wardour's future governor, who was at the siege, gives a slightly different version of events:

...there being a vault on each side of the castle, for the conveying away of filth, two or three barrels of powder were put into one of them, and being fired, blew up some part of it; which with the grazing of a bullet upon the face of one of the servants, and the threatening of the besiegers to spring the other mine, and then to storm it, if it was not surrendered before an hour-glass, which they had turn'd up, so terrified the ladies therein, whereof there was a great number, that they agreed to surrender it.

The Royalist newspaper claims that the Parliamentarians, in direct contravention of the agreed terms of surrender, then thoroughly looted and vandalised the castle and surrounding park causing damage which the Arundells later assessed at £100,000, and carried off five cartloads of loot together with Lady Blanche, her daughter-in-law and grandchildren. Soon after, Blanche was to receive the news that her husband had died of wounds received at the battle of Stratton on 15 May. Parliament placed Wardour under the command of Edmund Ludlow, a young Wiltshire officer who had fought at Edgehill in the lifeguard of the Earl of Essex and was later to become a leading Republican. Ludlow brought with him his own troop of cavalry (who were soon sent away as there was nowhere to stable their horses) and a company of infantry, about 100 men, under the command of a Captain Bean. He immediately set about trying to strengthen the defences of his new command:

I levelled the works that had been raised there during the siege, sunk a well, broke down the vaults about the castle, and furnished it with provisions, expecting to be besieged, as I was soon after. For within a fortnight after I was possessed of it, the Lord Arundell, to whom it belonged, and whose father died soon after he had received news that it was taken, supposing to find me unprovided, came with a party of horse, and summoned me to deliver the place for his Majesty's use. Some who were with me advised me to do so; yet I return'd the enemy answer, that I was entrusted to keep the castle for the service of the Parliament, and could not surrender it without their command. The enemy not being at that time ready to make any attempt upon us, retreated to their main body…

The capture of Wardour was a rare Parliamentarian victory in the south-west for the summer of 1643 had been a particularly successful one for the Royalists. Advancing from Cornwall under the command of Sir Ralph Hopton, they had defeated a Roundhead force at Stratton in April. On 13 July, after some tricky campaigning around Bath, they had (with the aid of reinforcements from Oxford) destroyed a Parliamentarian army under Sir William Waller at Roundway Down near Devizes. On 21 July they reoccupied Malmesbury and at the end of the month captured the vital port of Bristol. At Wardour, Ludlow was now in an extremely exposed and isolated position. The nearest friendly garrisons of any significance were Poole and Southampton, both over 35 miles away. Aware of this, Ludlow's father obtained an order from Parliament permitting his son to slight the castle and draw off his garrison for safety. But Ludlow was not going to give up without a fight, especially as Wardour was now the only Parliamentarian outpost in Wiltshire. Despite the fact that enemy forces were beginning to gather in the vicinity of the castle, Ludlow rode with a party of men to Southampton, returning with much-needed ammunition, and bolstered his supplies by intercepting produce being sent to market at Shaftesbury. According to Ludlow his men paid the going rate for the goods they seized, much to the surprise of their former owners. Eventually, in December 1643, a Royalist force arrived under Captain Christopher Bowyer, tasked with recapturing Wardour for Henry, the new Lord Arundell. Like his father, Henry had served with the western Royalists and had fought at the inconclusive battle of Lansdown where he had been wounded by two pistol shots in the thigh. How long the new owner of Wardour spent at the siege of his own castle is not known but he was certainly present at the final surrender negotiations, when he met with Edmund Ludlow.

Ludlow had not been able to build substantial defensive earthworks around the castle and in any case he did not have the troops to man them. His best hope of survival lay in the fact that the Royalists, who had bigger fish to fry, would be unlikely to divert substantial forces for the siege and that Lord Arundell was unlikely to wish to see significant damage caused to what was, after all, his own house. Indeed the Royalists' first attempt to recapture Wardour was by subterfuge. After a gun on Wardour's roof had mysteriously exploded as it was being fired at a Royalist raiding party, some of the garrison became suspicious of a 12-year-old boy who had recently been employed as the castle turnspit. Tying a length of matchcord around his neck and beginning to hoist him in the air on a halberd they threatened to hang him unless he told the truth. The frightened boy confessed all. He had been sent into the castle by the Royalists with instructions to find out the strength of the garrison, sabotage the castle guns, poison the water supply and blow up the ammunition. But Ludlow's men had also infiltrated the enemy camp. They had made contact with a reluctant Royalist soldier who had been pressed into service and persuaded him to signal to them if a relief force was approaching by blowing his nose on a white handkerchief.

The Royalists began operations by raising a breastwork on the hill overlooking the castle's main gate. From this vantage point they were able to pick off a number of defenders, including Ludlow's master gunner, as they dashed in and out of the castle to fetch wood. The siege began, as custom dictated, with the Royalists summoning the garrison to surrender and the Parliamentarians refusing. Ludlow describes the exchange:

> ...to get us out of the castle, [Bowyer] proposed to grant us what terms we desired; to which we replied, that we designed to discharge our duty by keeping it as long as we could. Upon this he threatened us with great numbers of horse and foot, attended with several pieces of cannon, which he said were drawing towards us...but Captain Bean told him that we were not at all affrighted with his menaces; but upon confidence of the justice of our cause, were resolved to defend the place to the utmost; and warning him to look to himself, fired a gun, with which he wounded him in the heel...

Bowyer soon succumbed to his wound and his place as commander of the besieging forces was taken by Colonel George Barnes whose brother, rather ironically, was chaplain to Ludlow's father. Ludlow was determined to be as active as possible in the defence of the castle. The Royalists had seized various outhouses surrounding the castle for use as observation posts but they were so close to the castle walls that they only used them at night. Knowing this, Ludlow planned an ambush, sending 'forty men through a vault leading to those houses, ordering them to lie private, and endeavour to surprise them when they came'. His plan would probably have worked had one of his men not fired his pistol the moment the first enemy came into view with the result that those following were warned and had the chance to escape.

Once again the Royalists tried to persuade Ludlow to surrender, sending a relative of Ludlow's from Oxford to discuss terms. Ludlow saw a chance to strengthen his bargaining position by misleading the besiegers about his strength:

> *I permitted him to come in, that seeing our strength and provision, he might make his report to the enemy to our advantage; for things were so ordered by removing our guards from place to place, filling up our hogsheads with empty barrels, and covering them with beef and pork, and in like manner ordering our corn, that everything seemed double to what it was.*

Ludlow followed this up by offering terms of surrender that he knew full well would be completely unacceptable to the Royalists. He said he would be prepared to leave the castle if he was not relieved in six months, but only if the Royalists would swear not to garrison it and would pay Parliament £2,000 compensation for the money they had spent capturing and defending it! His kinsman duly returned to Oxford with the offer but Ludlow received no reply. 'Neither did we expect any', was Ludlow's cynical observation. In fact Ludlow's position was nowhere near as strong as he had made out. Grain supplies were running low and all the castle's beer had been drunk, forcing the garrison to rely on water from a well that showed alarming signs of running dry. Nevertheless, determined to hold on for as long as possible, Ludlow reduced the rations of the hundred men of his garrison and began slaughtering captured horses to provide them with meat.

Throughout the siege Barnes's guns had bombarded the castle with little success but eventually a lucky shot broke the chain of the portcullis guarding the main gate, forcing the defenders to block up the entrance. As Wardour's other doors had already been walled up at the start of the siege the only way in or out of the castle for Ludlow's men was now through a window. However, as this was the only impression the besiegers' guns had actually made on the castle, the Royalists tried another tack and decided to attempt to undermine its walls. Taking advantage of the fact that Ludlow's men were in effect trapped inside the building, the Royalists sent forward parties of men at night with thick oak planks, with orders to lean them against the castle wall to create a shelter under which to work. One group was driven back by the fire of the defenders but a second party managed to reach the castle wall unnoticed. They built their wooden shelter and began chipping away at the foundations. Inside the castle Ludlow's men could hear the sound of digging but initially they were unable to see where it was coming from. Peering into the dark from the castle windows they eventually located the source of the noise and poured down boiling water and molten lead in a bid to drive off the attackers. At first the oak shelter did its job but in the end a barrage of hand grenades forced the Royalists to retreat, leaving their tools behind them.

By now two months had gone by and the Parliamentarians were still undefeated. In a bid to bring the siege to an end the Royalist leader in the south-west, Sir Ralph Hopton, sent the besiegers a party of miners from the Mendip Hills together with substantial reinforcements, all under the command of that uncompromising Cavalier, Sir Francis Doddington. Doddington's plan was to tunnel under the castle walls, plant barrels of gunpowder there and then force the Parliamentarians to surrender by blowing up the mine or at least threatening to do so. The Mendip miners began their work. When Ludlow's men heard the sound of tunnelling they attempted to dig a countermine of their own through which they could attack Doddington's miners. However, they were thwarted by the hardness of the castle foundations and presumably a lack of suitable tools. Warned by their nose-blowing spy that an attack was imminent, Ludlow's men stood to their arms for two nights. Finally, on 14 March 1644, events reached a literally explosive climax. Ludlow takes up the story:

...upon the Thursday morning, being very weary, I lay down and slept till between ten or eleven of the clock at which time one of my great guns firing upon the enemy shook the mach they had left burning for the springing of the mine into the powder, so that the mine springing I was lifted up with it from the floor, with much dust suddenly about me; which was no sooner laid but I found both the doors of my chamber blown open, and my window towards the enemy blown down, so that a cart might have entered at the breach.

To make matters worse, looking out through the gaping hole that was once his bedroom wall, Ludlow could see yellow-coated Royalist soldiers clambering up the rubble towards him. He reached for his pistols, only to find that they were useless.

My pistols being wheel-locks, and wound up all night, I could not get to fire, so that I was forced to trust to my sword for the keeping down of the enemy, being alone in the chamber, and all relief excluded from me, except such as came in by one of my windows that looked into the court of the castle...

After driving back his assailants with his sword Ludlow ran across his room to the window in order to call for help. A group of men hurried to his aid only to find that the ladder they were planning to use to climb up to Ludlow's window was nearly six feet too short! As a result Ludlow was forced to dash to and fro across his room, first holding off his attackers, then running back to help his rescuers climb up through the courtyard window. Eventually, aided by his comrades, Ludlow was able to barricade the hole in his wall with his bed and other pieces of furniture and then climb out of his room to inspect the damage caused to the castle by the exploding mine. He cannot have liked what he saw. The west side of the castle was badly cracked, two of its turrets had collapsed, numerous doorways and windows had caved in and the guns he had mounted on the roof had crashed to the ground. To make matters worse a substantial proportion of his supplies and ammunition had also been destroyed in the blast. Ludlow knew that time was running out. The castle's defences had been seriously weakened and even if his men were able to keep the Royalists at bay, a shortage of supplies meant that surrender was inevitable. It was now just a question of getting the best terms he could. Some of those in the castle wanted to treat with the Royalists immediately. But Ludlow was keen to hold out a little longer, arguing that a show of resistance might improve the terms of surrender offered to them:

I thought it advisable, having repulsed the enemy, to put the best countenance we could upon our affairs, hoping by so doing we might bring the enemy to give us the better conditions... if we should now desire a treaty with them, they would conclude our spirits low, our condition desperate, and so hold us to harder terms, or it may be give us none at all.

In the end Ludlow gave way and allowed his subordinates to ask for a parley with the Royalists to discuss terms of surrender. But the Royalists, who knew full well they now had the upper hand, were having none of it and, as Ludlow had feared, initially refused to offer any terms at all. Soon after, however, a truce was agreed and negotiations began with Ludlow offering to surrender the castle if he and his men were permitted to march away with their arms and belongings to the nearest Parliamentarian garrison. Hardly surprisingly, this was refused. Ludlow, who had briefly considered leading a night-time breakout from the castle, then offered to hand himself over to the Royalists if his men were allowed to go free. But his bargaining position was anything but strong – the castle was barely defensible, provisions were exhausted, morale was low and there was no prospect of relief. On 18 March Ludlow finally reached an agreement with Doddington and Lord Arundell, who had returned to take possession of his now ruined home. Ludlow sums up the terms of surrender:

> I told them, that unless I might have four things granted I would not deliver the castle. 1st. Quarter without distinction for the lives of everyone. 2ndly. Civil usage for all my party. 3rdly. Not to be carried to Oxford. 4thly. A speedy exchange. They promised me I should have these terms to the full... Thus all things being agreed upon I returned to the castle and ordered my men to lay down their arms.

Initially Ludlow and his men were treated well by the victorious Royalists although he later complained that his sick and wounded were kept for some time in the castle's hall where 'a Popish priest very solemnly, with his hands spread over them, cursed them three times'. However, among the prisoners were two men who had been pressed into the Royalist army but had later changed sides. When Ludlow heard that Doddington was planning to execute them despite the fact that the terms of surrender granted quarter for all, a furious argument broke out over their fates. Captain Leicester, a Cavalier officer from Ireland, insisted that the two men were part of the Royalist army. As such, he argued, they were for the Royalists to do with as they pleased and that if Ludlow had intended to have them included in the original agreement then he should have made a point of naming them. Despite Ludlow's protests that 'Quarter without distinction' meant just that, they were taken away, condemned and put to death.

Despite the terms of his surrender, Ludlow was sent to Oxford along with his men, but he was quickly exchanged for a Royalist prisoner and commissioned by Sir William Waller to raise a regiment of horse. In July he crossed swords with Sir Francis Doddington for a second time and once again he came off second best. Doddington was besieging Woodhouse Manor near Longleat, which was defended by Major Edward Wansey, a watchmaker from Bristol. Ironically, Woodhouse was another of Lord Arundell's houses, captured by the Parliamentarians in the previous year. Ludlow set off with a relief party but was routed by Doddington on Warminster Heath and chased to Southampton. Doddington then brought up some heavy guns and soon breached the walls of the house, forcing Wansey to surrender on 17 July 1644. In reprisal for the execution by the Parliamentarians of some Irish Royalist prisoners, Doddington then hanged a dozen of the defenders on a tree outside the house. Described by the Parliamentarians as 'an intransigent and bullying Royalist', Doddington was nonetheless an extremely effective soldier. Indeed, the surrender of the Earl of Essex's Parliamentarian army at Lostwithiel on 1 September 1644 was in part due to Doddington's defeat of General Middleton's relief force in Somerset two weeks earlier. Following Parliament's victory and the execution of the king in 1649, he was one of 12 leading Royalists who were declared enemies and traitors to the Commonwealth, had their estates confiscated and were banished from the country.

In April 1645 Ludlow resigned his command and the following year became MP for Wiltshire. In 1649 he sat on the High Court of Justice that tried and condemned the king and was one of those who signed King Charles's death warrant. He took up arms again in 1650, campaigning in Ireland and briefly serving as commander-in-chief there following the death of Cromwell's son-in-law, Henry Ireton. He bitterly clashed with Cromwell following the latter's seizure of power, believing that the new Lord Protector had betrayed the principles for which they had both fought. After the Restoration, Ludlow fled to the continent with a price on his head. He lived quietly at Vevey, where he was joined by his wife in 1663. He briefly returned to England in 1689 after the Glorious Revolution, but when an order was issued for his arrest as an attainted traitor he returned once again to Vevey. When he died there, in November 1692, he was probably the last surviving regicide.

chapter ten

Terms of Surrender

L udlow's experiences at Wardour clearly demonstrate that negotiating the surrender of a fortress was one of the trickiest aspects of 17th-century warfare. An attacking force would normally begin a siege by 'summoning' a town or fortress, offering the defenders certain concessions to persuade them to surrender. What these concessions actually were tended to vary according to circumstance. In order to bring things to a rapid conclusion or to avoid heavy casualties, the attackers might offer the defenders full 'honours of war' – the right to march out with drums beating, music playing, colours flying, carrying all their arms and equipment and to join their main army. In 1651, for example, wishing to avoid a costly seaborne assault, Admiral Blake offered the Royalist defenders of the Scilly island of St Mary's particularly generous terms of surrender. The Royalists were to be allowed to depart with their weapons and property, the Irish to Ireland, the English to join Charles II in Scotland and Blake would supply a vessel to help the Royalists carry away their supplies. Sir John Grenville, The Royalist governor, was to go free and Blake even agreed to compensate him for some guns he had purchased for the defence of the island but would be forced to leave behind!

However, if a siege had dragged on, casualties had been heavy or the besiegers felt confident of success, the defenders might have to surrender without any conditions at all. Indeed, according to the 'laws of war' of the period, if the defenders forced the attackers to storm a place then their lives were forfeit if it fell. Although on the face of it this custom may seem barbaric, it was in fact intended to prevent what was called at the time 'the unnecessary effusion of blood' by defenders who inflicted heavy casualties on an attacking force then sought to surrender at the last minute. Sir Anthony Ashley Cooper

Three stages of a siege – negotiation (left), escalade (centre) and mining (right), from a late 14th-century manuscript.

Artist's impression of a trebuchet.

A 14th-century depiction of miners at work under the cover of a mobile shelter. The defenders hurl down missiles, rocks and Greek fire.

Norman soldiers force the surrender of Dinan by setting fire to its timber walls, in a scene from the Bayeux Tapestry.

A 15th-century woodcut of a trebuchet in action, watched by an apprehensive spectator. As one of William the Lion's knights discovered to his cost in 1174, it was advisable to stand well clear.

Soldiers looting, an all-too-common occurrence on both sides of the Anglo-Scottish border during the medieval and Tudor periods.

Prudhoe Castle, which withstood sieges in 1173 and 1174.

Brough Castle, captured by William the Lion in 1174.

Rochester Castle keep. The round corner tower is a replacement for the square one brought down in 1215.

Artist's impression of undermining at Dover's outer gate in 1216.

Dover Castle. The original gatehouse stood behind the round tower in the centre of the picture. Its replacement, the Constable's Gate, is to the right.

Medieval tunnel at Dover Castle.

Kenilworth Castle from the Mere.

Artist's impression of Kenilworth at the time of the siege, 1266.

Two trebuchets bombard a castle while a defender retaliates with a slightly less lethal projectile.

Margaret of Anjou, the driving force behind Lancastrian resistance in Northumberland after their defeat at Towton in 1461.

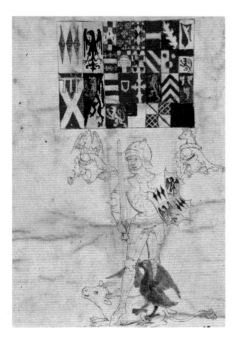

Richard Neville, Earl of Warwick, commander of Yorkist forces in the north 1461–64.

A 15th-century illustration showing the effects of an artillery bombardment on a city.

Alnwick Castle.

Dunstanburgh Castle.

Bamburgh Castle.

Norham Castle, overlooking the Tweed and the border with Scotland.

The Tudor earthworks at Norham, constructed after the siege of 1513.

16th-century woodcut showing miners at work, while cannons bombard a fortress from behind the cover of earth-filled baskets known as gabions.

Tudor drawing of an English army on the march, possibly Henry VIII's expedition to France in 1513. Screened by cavalry, the army is accompanied by guns, baggage wagons, camp followers and livestock which will be slaughtered to feed the soldiers.

Civil War propaganda – the Royalist newspaper *Mercurius Rusticus* depicting scenes from the Civil War.

Having fixed a petard to a gate, a 17th-century soldier lights the fuse – and beats a hasty retreat.

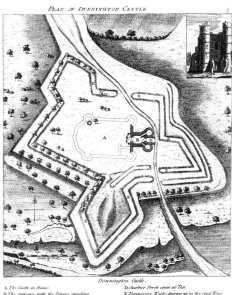

18th-century plan of Donnington Castle showing the civil war earthworks around the remains of the medieval castle.

Edmund Ludlow, Parliamentarian governor of Wardour Castle in 1644.

Victorian engraving showing the defence of Wardour by Blanche Arundell and her servants.

Wardour Castle today. Bullet marks are still visible around some of the windows.

The interior of Wardour showing the damage caused when the Royalist mine exploded.

The siege of Corfe Castle, after a contemporary engraving.

The ruins of Corfe.

Corfe's defender, Lady Mary Bankes.

Brilliana Harley of Brampton Bryan Castle.

Sir William Brereton. Despite his glum expression, Brereton was one of Parliament's most energetic commanders.

Part of the inner ward of Beeston Castle.

Goodrich Castle from the air. John Birch sited his artillery near the top of the picture.

Goodrich Castle from the west, with the keep in the background.

Goodrich, with the south-west tower in the foreground.

Roaring Meg, the mortar that Birch had specially cast for use against Goodrich.

Pendennis Castle from the west, across Falmouth Bay.

Pendennis Castle showing the Elizabethan and Stuart defences that were built around Henry VIII's castle.

'Little Dennis', a Tudor blockhouse built at sea level.

An artist's impression of Pendennis during the siege of 1646.

recalled that when in 1644 he summoned the Royalist garrison of Abbotsbury to surrender:

they returned a slighting answer and hung out their bloody flag…After this we sent them a second summons under our hands, that they might have fair quarter if they would accept it, otherwise they must accept none if they forced us to storm… But they were so gallant that they would admit of no treaty, so that we prepared ourselves for to force it, and accordingly fell on.

Cooper's men

…set the whole house in a flaming fire so that it was not possible to be quenched, and then they cried for quarter; but we having lost divers men before it, and considering how many garrisons of the same nature we were to deal with, I gave command there should be none given, but that they should be kept into the house, that they and their garrison might fall together.

In the event, Cooper's second-in-command Colonel William Sydenham ignored his order and instructed his men to spare the garrison. Indeed it was the Parliamentarians who suffered further casualties when the house blew up while they were looting it.

Although wholesale massacres were rare in civil war England, they did take place. After Sir Michael Woodhouse captured Hopton Castle from the Parliamentarians in 1643 he had the garrison executed; the slaughter of defenders in the heat of the moment certainly happened on numerous occasions. When Basing House, the Hampshire stronghold of the Marquess of Winchester, was stormed by Cromwell's troops in 1645, many of its defenders were put to the sword. Sir William Brereton gently reminded Lord Byron, the Royalist governor of Chester, of this when summoning him to surrender in 1646:

I shall offer to your consideration the example of Liverpool, Basing and Lathom, which by their refusal of honourable terms when they were propounded, were not long after subjected to captivity and the sword.

Whether the defenders accepted the terms that were offered to them also depended on circumstance. Any governor who surrendered too quickly risked incurring the wrath of his senior commanders, so at least some show of resistance was required. Captain Thomas Steele, the Parliamentarian governor of Beeston Castle in Cheshire, discovered this to his cost in December 1643. Returning to Roundhead Nantwich after surrendering the castle to a minute force of Royalists, he was court-martialled and executed, shot by firing squad against the wall of St Mary's Church. The same fate befell the Royalist Colonel Francis Windebank, shot in Oxford in May 1645 for surrendering Bletchingdon House to Cromwell without offering any resistance. As a result a governor would normally reject an initial summons to surrender, often with a suitably defiant answer. 'You are not now at Bletchingdon', was Colonel Burges's acerbic reply when summoned by Cromwell to surrender nearby Faringdon Castle.

If, however, a castle or town's defences were in ruins, there was no prospect of relief, or his garrison was starving, a governor who had put up a good fight could normally surrender with his honour intact, having first obtained the best terms he could for both himself and his men. Negotiations could drag on for months with the terms that each side was prepared to offer and accept often changing as a siege developed and besieger or besieged gained a new advantage. Defenders frequently spun out negotiations for as long as possible to save ammunition and in the hope that if they held on long enough they might be rescued by a relieving force.

Of course when a garrison did surrender there was no guarantee that the victorious besiegers would actually honour the terms that had been agreed. Wardour Castle is a case in point. The Parliamentarians thoroughly looted the place in May 1643 despite having agreed to respect the property of its owners and, according to Edmund Ludlow at least, the Royalists were none too scrupulous about observing the terms under which he surrendered the castle back to them in 1644. On the whole, however, agreements were honoured. Commanders knew that failure to do so could lead to reprisals elsewhere and might make other fortresses and towns less willing to surrender in the future.

chapter eleven

Beeston 1643–45

uilt on a rocky crag nearly 500ft above the Cheshire plain, Beeston Castle commanded a major route from the plain into the Midlands through a gap in the hills that stretches north–south through the county. Its strong defensive position and strategic importance had long been appreciated; archaeologists have uncovered evidence of both a Bronze Age community and an Iron Age fort. In 1225 Ranulf, Earl of Chester, began the construction of a stone castle on the site. Known in medieval times as *Castellum de Rupe*, 'the castle of the rock', its defences were formidable. A large outer ward on the lower slopes of the hill was enclosed by a curtain wall with towers and a fortified gatehouse. On the summit of the crag stood the compact inner ward, also defended by towers and a gatehouse and with the additional natural protection of precipitous cliffs to the north, east and west, supplemented by a deep rock-hewn ditch to the south. The castle was taken into royal hands in 1237 and was maintained primarily as a supply depot and occasional prison, but by the 17th century it had fallen into disuse and disrepair. The Tudor historian William Camden had described the castle as 'a place well guarded by walls of a great compass, by a great number of towers and by a mountain of steep ascent' but, according to Nathaniel Lancaster, chaplain to Parliament's forces in Cheshire, by 1642 Beeston was 'no more than the skeleton or bare anatomy of a castle'.

Despite its apparent disrepair, for a while after the outbreak of civil war in England in 1642, Beeston, like so many other medieval castles across the country, found a new lease of life. In February 1643 it was seized by Sir William Brereton, the energetic commander of Parliament's forces in Cheshire. Installing a garrison of about 200 men in the castle he ordered the gaps in its walls to be filled with mud, the well in the outer ward to be cleared out, and erected wooden stables, stores and barracks in the outer ward. But as the year went on and Brereton's men gained the upper hand in the county, Beeston's military importance declined. With its garrison cut to about 60 men the castle was once again used simply as a supply depot and a place where Parliamentarian supporters could safely store their property. Garrison duty in such a tedious military backwater was not a popular posting for Roundhead officers who hoped to further their military careers, and eventually the castle was placed in the care of a Captain Thomas Steele, who in civilian life had been a cheese-monger from Nantwich. A contemporary later wrote:

> A captain or two being wearied out of the charge of such a prison, it was committed to Captain Steele (a rough-hewn man; no soldier) whose care was more to see it repaired, victualled and live quietly there, than the safe custody of it.

Steele took up residence in the castle's outer gatehouse but his quiet life there was soon to be rudely interrupted. In November 1643 Sir John Byron, reinforced by five regiments of veteran troops from the king's army in Ireland, mounted a major counter-offensive in Cheshire and North Wales and on the night of 12 December a Royalist force arrived at Beeston. Led by Captain Thomas Sandford, a hard-bitten officer from the army in Ireland, it consisted of some companies of foot from Sir Francis Gamul's regiment together with some 'firelocks' from Sandford's own regiment. In this context a firelock was a soldier armed with a flintlock musket, a weapon that was fired by the sparks caused when its flint struck steel. It was considerably less complicated to fire than the matchlocks with which the majority of musketeers were equipped and was therefore an ideal weapon to carry in an assault. The flintlock had the added advantage that it did not give away the position of its owner at night, unlike the matchlock which was fired by a piece of constantly smouldering cord (*see* Appendices). The Royalists soon got the better of Steele. According to the Royalist newspaper *Mercurius Aulicus*:

> Lord Byron sent out the firelocks and about 200 commanded musketeers to Beeston Castle... and having two men to be their guide that had formerly been very conversant in the castle, assaulted the outer ward, and presently forced the entrance, after that they fell upon the river [inner]

ward (where the greater part of their provision and all their ammunition was stored up) and very courageously soon made themselves masters of it...

A Parliamentarian account states that:

a little before day, and after the moon was set, Capt Sandford and eight of his firelocks got into the upper ward of Beeston Castle, by a byeway, through treachery it is supposed...

Exactly how they managed to do this is not known. It has been suggested that they scaled the northern face of the crag where the castle wall was much lower because the gradient of the cliff on that side was considered adequate defence in itself. However no contemporary account of the capture of the castle actually states this. One suggestion is that while Gamul's men staged a diversion in front of the lower gatehouse, Sandford and his firelocks were shown a way into the outer bailey of the castle by the two men mentioned in *Mercurius Aulicus* and then rushed the gatehouse of the inner bailey. With both the inner bailey and most of his ammunition now in the hands of his enemies, Steele decided to sue for terms and, having handed the castle over to the Royalists, returned with his men to the Parliamentarian headquarters at Nantwich. The Roundhead commanders there were not amused. The fact that Steele had surrendered Beeston almost without a fight was bad enough but matters were made worse by the fact that many of their personal possessions were in it at the time. Reports that Steele had entertained Sandford to dinner prior to surrendering, and had also sent copious supplies of beer to the Royalists in the upper bailey, were the last straw. He was court-martialled, sentenced to death and shot by two musketeers in Tynker's Croft behind St Mary's Church in Nantwich.

Now in the hands of the king, Beeston joined the castles of Holt and Hawarden as one of the outlying garrisons defending the approaches to the important Royalist port of Chester. Archaeological excavations carried out between 1968 and 1985 suggest that the Royalists made further improvements to its defences, altering arrow loops, creating gunports and possibly strengthening some of the walls in the inner bailey. (Brereton was later to comment that the Royalists had 'well strengthened' the castle.) The discovery of two large post holes suggests that the outer gatehouse, which was probably protected by the construction of some rudimentary earthworks, was fitted with a new wooden gate. Seventeenth-century clay pipes, pottery and coins have been found throughout the castle and the fact that the pottery in the upper gate-house is of a higher quality than that found elsewhere may indicate that this was the location of the officers' quarters. The Parliamentarians regained the initiative in Cheshire following Sir Thomas Fairfax's victory over Byron at Nantwich in January 1644 but Beeston remained largely undisurbed until November when Brereton's troops laid siege to Chester. Beeston's dangerous position, to the rear of the besieging army's headquarters, meant it could not be ignored, so it was invested at the same time. The Parliamentarians do not seem to have made any serious attempts to storm the castle. Instead their objective was to bottle up the garrison, prevent it from mounting raids and ultimately starve it into submission by denying it supplies. Brereton's troops began operations by rounding up a number of the garrison cattle which were grazing outside the castle and fighting off a Royalist attempt to recover them. After two more successful cattle-rustling raids Brereton tightened the net around Beeston by ordering the occupation of a number of nearby farms and houses in order to establish a series of outposts around the castle. On 7 December the defenders hit back. Forty to fifty men slipped out of the castle and surprised a party of 26 Parliamentarians who were dining in a house at the foot of the hill. After setting fire to the house they killed 24 of the men and took the remaining two back to the castle as prisoners. Despite this setback and outbreaks of discontent amongst his men, many of whom had not been paid, Brereton was confident of success. In January 1645 he wrote to Parliament's Committee of Both Kingdoms that 'Beeston Castle is every day more and more distressed' and the following month reported that 'we still maintain the siege of Beeston Castle, which we hope cannot hold out long'. However, on 19 February a Royalist force under the command of Prince Maurice relieved Chester and a month later, reinforced by more troops under Maurice's elder brother Prince Rupert, they marched on Beeston and replenished its supplies. One of Rupert's officers wrote in his diary:

> the enemy, having intelligence of our intention to relieve Beeston, quitted the siege; left their works undemolished and a sow behind them... 8,000 weight of biscuit; plenty of beef, only some want of fire and beer.

Evidence of the hardening of attitudes on both sides by this stage of the war can be seen in a slightly later entry where he records that:

*this day at the rendezvous we hanged the 12 prisoners taken on Monday
all on one crabtree, they having formerly served his Majesty and we being
invited thereunto by their examples at Shrewsbury.*

His final comment refers to the execution of a number of Royalist prisoners after the capture of Shrewsbury in accordance with Parliament's ordinance
that all native Irish soldiers captured in this country were to be put to death.
During the spring of 1645 both sides carried out a number of executions and
on 12 April 1645 Major Thomas Croxton, the governor of Nantwich, was
unhappy to receive an order from Brereton instructing him to hang some
prisoners from Beeston. He replied:

*I received a command from you for the executing of some of Beeston's
soldiers. I could have wished that no quarter had been given to them that
were first taken, but having quarter given to them I know of no order or
ordinance that authorises the taking away of their lives. But if you please
to send a warrant to the marshal I shall see it put into execution. They that
were taken last were pressed for pioneers and had overrun [deserted] the
castle since the raising of the siege. Therefore I conceive the giving of
quarter to them was fit. The castle soldiers have taken divers of our men
prisoners since theirs were taken, who must expect no more mercy than we
intend to them. I refer this to your further order.*

It is not known whether the prisoners in question were Irish or whether
Brereton's order was in reprisal for the hanging of the 12 Parliamentarian
prisoners after Rupert's relief of Beeston. In any event it seems that Croxton's
arguments prevailed and the lives of the men were spared, though sporadic
executions of prisoners who were Irish or thought to be Irish continued
throughout the war.

Unfortunately for the Cheshire Royalists, Rupert and Maurice were soon
needed elsewhere and when troops left the area the Parliamentarians resumed
the siege of Chester and blockade of Beeston. On 8 May Brereton reported:

*We have almost finished a mount before Beeston Castle gate, which is
encompassed with a strong, deep trench. This will command and keep
them in the castle, so that they dare not issue out in strong parties to annoy
the country or bring in provisions.*

It seems that the Parliamentarians were planning to burn down a house near the castle, because on 9 May 1645 Captain William Vallet, the Royalist governor of Beeston, penned a letter to Captain Godfrey Gimbart who seems to have been in charge of the siege operations. Vallet was a professional soldier who had previously served in Lord Byron's regiment of horse while Gimbart appears to have been an officer in one of the regiments from Ireland that changed sides following their defeat at Nantwich in 1644. The ensuing correspondence between the two soldiers is in marked contrast to the polite formality of the letters exchanged at Goodrich by Birch and Lingen (*see* chapter 14). Vallet wrote:

> *I understand by the bearer that you intend to burn the house. Indeed it should not have been left for you to have done it, but that I did commiserate a poor widow and two poor orphans in so much that I was content rather than to shew that extremity to suffer it to be a den of thieves and traitors. But if you take this course you prevent that which I might, upon good reasons, do myself and I shall make it such a precedent as the surveyors of your works – Aldersey, Spurstowe, Metcalfe cum multiis aliis of your traitorous faction shall repent. And whereas you flatter yourself with hopes of taking this place, I scorn your threats and attempts and the forces of your best general, for all his great ram's head.*

Not to be outdone, Gimbart replied:

> *From my royal fort which stands for the confusion of a den of traitors in Beeston Castle. Governor, I have received your civil expressions in a scandalous paper. You said you delighted in civility; it appears in your beastlike expressions. You told me you would not be tied to conditions. And do you think to tie [me] that am at liberty, and that by you whom I keep close prisoner amongst your anti-Christian, Babylonian crew and will wait to expend my dearest blood upon the destruction of such traitors to King and state as that den of blasphemers are whereof you are chief. You cause me to burn the house by your expressions...*
>
> *For your scandals to my general, you put it upon him whose shoes you are not worthy to clean. But I suppose you take the counsel to write this letter with the asses whom you took prisoners.*

Within a few days the Parliamentarians were once again forced to raise the siege of Beeston, this time on the approach of the king's main field army which had begun the campaign that would end in disaster at Naseby on 14 June. In late July, however, the blockade of the castle was once again resumed. In the absence of Brereton, who had been temporarily recalled to London, it was left to two able subordinates, Colonels Michael Jones and James Lothian, to take charge of operations. They began by completing the fort that Brereton had begun building in May. Constructed 'within musket shot of the castle before the gate', it contained a storehouse for provisions and ammunition, and was linked to a trench, or counterscarffe, which cut the castle off from the outside world. Inevitably the defenders of Beeston began to run out of food and the fact that the remains of pigs, sheep and cattle found during archaeological excavations included a high proportion of younger animals suggests that the hungry garrison had been forced to slaughter and eat them before they would normally have done. After the major Parliamentarian victory at Rowton Heath outside Chester on 24 September Beeston's fate was sealed, and on 13 November Vallet asked the besiegers for terms of surrender. However, during the negotiations the Parliamentarians received worrying news – the Royalists at Chirk and Holt had somehow managed to organise a relief force which was on its way to Beeston with supplies of meat and cheese. Thinking that their work was done the Parliamentarians outside Beeston had somewhat relaxed their guard, and letters were hurriedly sent to them warning them to prepare for an attack and a possible sortie from Beeston. As Brereton later put it:

...our guards about the castle were not in so good a condition as were to be desired, very many of our men being straggled abroad, secure upon the confidence of the castle being [about] to be delivered up the next day. Hence it came to pass that we were constrained to send to Nantwich [for] our town company and to the horse quarters whose remoteness did induce us to suspect that they might not come in time.

Anxious to secure the surrender of the castle before the Royalist relief force could arrive, the Parliamentarians offered more generous terms to the defenders than originally intended. The official terms of surrender were as follows:

Articles of agreement for the surrender of Beeston Castle concluded between Colonel Thomas Croxton and Lieut Colonel Chidley Coote for

Sir William Brereton and Captain Robert Barrow and Mr William Smith for Captain William Vallet, governor of Beeston Castle.

1. Tomorrow, 16-11-45, before 10am the castle shall be delivered up to Brereton or whosoever he shall appoint, with all arms, ammunition and goods, except such be excepted by these articles and, whether or not the garrison shall have marched out by the hour appointed, they shall suffer a guard of 200 musketeers appointed by Brereton to take possession of both upper and lower wards of the said castle.

2. No arms that are agreed on to be left behind shall be hid, made away with or impaired, no ammunition spoiled or mispent, none of the goods embezzled, roofs or any part of the castle defaced, nor either of the wells poisoned or obstructed.

3. The convoy sent with them with their safety shall safely return.

4. Capts Vallet and Barrow with all their officers and soldiers shall march away from the said castle with complete arms, drums beating and colours flying, to Flint Castle and from thence to Beaumaris, as shall seem best to them, each soldier with three shots of powder and lighted matches and bullets answerable.

5. Capts Vallet and Barrow with all the rest of the gents and officers shall carry away their trunks, their wearing clothes and proper goods, leaving behind all such goods as truly belong to the said garrison and country, and the soldiers shall march away with their wearing apparel, whatever the apparel shall be, and all their proper monies.

6. All such gents, officers and soldiers and others, as have a desire or resolution to submit themselves to king and parliament and to live at home peaceably and quietly in their own houses, shall have free liberty and passes to such places as they desire to repair unto.

7. Capts Vallett and Barrow and the rest of the officers and soldiers and all that belong unto them shall have a safe convoy two miles beyond Flint and a trumpet, if he be required, to Denbigh or Rhuddlan, and two carriages by the aforementioned time to carry their aforesaid goods.

The 'said garrison' in point 5 refers to Steele's previous garrison at Beeston; because the local Parliamentarians had used Beeston as a storehouse for their valuables, now that the castle was about to surrender many had turned up there in the hope of recovering their property. Nathaniel Lancaster later wrote:

*their march out being on the Sabbath occasioned the breach of that holy
rest to many in the country, who attended their first opportunity to enquire
after their plundered goods.*

At midnight on 16 November Vallet and his soldiers marched out of
Beeston. In a letter to the Commitee of Both Kingdoms Brereton reported:

*The Lord hath been pleased this day to restore unto us the strong castle of
Beeston which was lost about this time two years and besieged by me this
day twelvemonth. Since which time they have had no more liberty but
what was obtained first by Rupert's and Maurice's army in March last
which raised us from that siege; which, being after their return made good,
we were again disturbed the second time by the king's army which came
within ten miles of Nantwich as he marched towards Leicester.*

*We found in the castle about 80 arms, some little ammunition but less
provision. The Gov Capt Vallet, with about 50 of the soldiers, was
permitted to march away on foot with their arms to Flint and so to
Denbigh or Beaumaris. There remained about 40, who laid down their
arms and submitted themselves, desiring liberty to live at home.*

*The prize therein found being of very small value... is with equality to be
distributed amongst the soldiers who have performed a very tedious siege...
We found their horses in a weak and languishing condition, the governor's
own horse being scarcely able to go out of the castle. We were very exact in
performing and making good the conditions agreed upon, which we hope
may produce a good effect upon Chester...*

Another Parliamentarian writer claimed that when Brereton's men entered
the castle there was

*...neither meat, ale, nor beer found in the castle; save only a piece of turkey
pie, two biscuits, a live peacock and a peahen.*

This is often cited as evidence of the reduced state of the Beeston garrison,
though it is tempting to speculate that the Royalists, knowing they were about
to surrender, would have made a hearty feast of their remaining provisions,

if only to prevent them from falling into the hands of their enemies. Vallett led the soldiers who remained with him to Denbigh, where he remained until its surrender the following year. Brereton ordered the dismantling of the siege-works surrounding Beeston and placed a garrison inside the castle itself. On 3 February 1646 Chester finally surrendered to the Parliamentarians; there was now no military reason to continue to garrison Beeston, other than to prevent any diehard Royalists from reoccupying it. That spring the garrison was withdrawn and Parliament gave orders for the castle's demolition.

Postscript: the miserable effects of war

This petition, typical of many made at the time, is a poignant reminder of the human cost of the war, not only to the soldiers who did the fighting but also to the families who were left behind. It almost certainly refers to the incident of 7 December 1644 when 26 Parliamentarian soldiers were trapped in a house near the castle and all but but two of them killed.

To the worshipful Committee or the Several Justices of Peace, whom this may concern.

The Humble Petition of Thomas Collier of the Parish of Mottram in Longdendale.

Most humbly showeth unto your Worships that your petitioner Thomas Collier, a poor inhabitant near Mottram in Longdendale, has been a great pains taker and lived in good repute, by the trade of a woollen webster, and now through age and infirmity is not able any longer to maintain himself and wife being either of them four score years of age or thereabouts, and as it has pleased the Lord to add more sorrow unto his old age, had two sons quartered or listed under the command of Col Dukenfield from in the beginning, and in the last siege at Beeston Castle were in their sentry house run through and utterly burned and consumed to ashes, which were the only stay and relief for him and their present maintenance. The one son, being married, having a wife and two small children, the wife's heart was burst and as it apparently appeared died for grief, and has left the two small children upon the charge of the two old people who have not any maintenance for themselves but lie languishing under most miserable conditions for the present.

May I therefore please the worshipful Committee or the Several Justices of peace, whom this may concern, taking into serious consideration the most miserable sad and weak condition of this poor supplicant that some speedy order might be taken for relief of himself, wife and two small father and motherless children that lie upon his hands through the barbarous cruelty of those wicked murders; and your petitioner shall and will be bound over continually to pray.

ENDORSED: The contents of this petition I believe to be true my hand this 29 March 1650.
Robert Dukenfield (Signed also by John Vryton, John Hollinworth, John Hollinworth Jnr and John Etchells)

ENDORSED: The substance of this petition I do believe to be truth and therefore do conceive it to be a work of mercy to allow the said petitioner and orphans above mentioned some relief, either out of the assessments for maimed soldiers widows and orphans or otherwise as your worships shall think fit.

Francis Shelmerdine, Pastor of Mottram

chapter twelve

Corfe 1643–46

There is in the Isle of Purbeck a strong castle called Corfe Castle, seated on a very steep hill, in the fracture of a hill in the very midst of it, being eight miles in length, running from the east end of the peninsula to the west; and though it stands between the two ends of this fracture, so that it might seem to lose much advantage of its natural and artificial strength as commanded from thence, being of height equal to, if not overlooking the tops of the highest towers of the castle; yet the structure of the castle is so strong, the ascent is so steep, the walls so massive and thick, that it is one of the impregnablest forts in the kingdom, and of very great concernment in respect of its command over the island and the places about it.

Mercurius Rusticus 1646

Standing on a site that had been occupied since Saxon times, Corfe Castle served as a royal fortress, palace and prison from the reign of William the Conqueror until 1572 when it was sold by Elizabeth I to Sir Christopher Hatton, her future Chancellor. In 1635 the castle was bought by Sir John Bankes, one of the country's leading lawyers. As Charles I's Attorney-General, Bankes was closely involved in some of the most celebrated legal cases of the time and found legal precedents to enable Charles I to raise money without recourse to Parliament. He also oversaw the famous trial for libel of Prynne, Bastwick and Burton in 1637 and, in the same year, represented the Crown in the prosecution of John Hampden for his refusal to pay Ship Money. Created Lord Chief Justice of the Common Pleas in January 1641, he joined the king at York in 1642 where he was made a member of the Privy Council, and at the end of that year followed him to Oxford. When war broke out in August 1642, despite his track record as an instrument of what some might have considered to have been the arbitrary exercise of royal power, Bankes was seen by many Parliamentarians as a voice of moderation. Indeed, the peace proposals present-ed to Charles I by Parliament in February 1643 included a specific request that he should remain in office. Bankes's reputation as a potential peacemaker may explain why the Dorset Parliamentarians left Corfe alone until May of that year.

Inevitably attitudes were to harden as the war went on. In 1644 a number of leading Parliamentarians were indicted *in absentia* for treason by Bankes and three other judges, and Parliament responded by impeaching the four judges, also for treason. Safe in Oxford, Bankes was out of their reach, but Parliament nevertheless ordered the seizure of his estates, goods and even his law books. Bankes had married Mary, the only daughter of Ralph Hawtrey of Ruislip in Middlesex. While Bankes joined the king at the outbreak of hostilities, his wife retired to Corfe with their numerous children and initially lived there unmolested. However, Corfe's commanding position meant that it would not be left alone indefinitely. By May 1643 most of Dorset was under Parliamentarian control but Purbeck would never be truly secure while the castle remained in Royalist hands, and Purbeck was important not least because of the sheltered anchorages around its shores. Writing 60 years earlier Elizabeth I's chief minister Lord Burghley had noted that:

At Studland Bay forty boats may land; at Swanwich and Studland may ride 600 or 700 sail of ships, of a 1,000 ton, almost in all winds; there is good landing almost three miles at Worbarrow Bay, and Shipman's Pool may ride about 500 sail of a 1,000 ton, in most winds.

The Roundheads' first attempt to capture the castle came on 1 May 1643 when a group of Parliamentarian supporters tried to surprise Lady Bankes and her supporters during the traditional Corfe May Day stag hunt:

On this day some troopes of horse from Dorchester and other places came into the island, intending to find other game than to hunt the stagge, their business being suddenly to surprise the gentleman in the hunting and to take the castle.

However Lady Bankes got wind of the scheme. The hunt was called off and the castle gates firmly closed against all-comers. A few days later, in an attempt to render Corfe defenceless, 40 seamen from Parliamentarian Poole arrived at the castle early in the morning with a warrant for the seizure of four small guns that had been set up in the castle. According to *Mercurius Rusticus*:

> *the Lady in person (early as it was) goes to the gates and desires to see their warrant; they produce one… but, instead of delivering them, though at that time there were but five men in the castle, yet these five, assisted by the maid-servants at their lady's command, mount these pieces on their carriages… and loading one of them they gave fire, which small thunder so affrighted the sea-men that they all quitted the place and ran away.*

Until now Lady Bankes had been attempting to keep a low profile, arguing that she needed the guns for her personal protection, but now the game was up. Knowing that it was only a matter of time before a larger Parliamentarian force arrived on the scene, she called for help amongst her tenants and friends, who joined her inside the castle. The Parliamentarians responded by blockading Corfe, intercepting a consignment of gunpowder intended for its defence and forbidding local markets to sell it any supplies. Even more effective, however, was the Parliamentarian threat to burn down the homes of those who had rallied to Lady Bankes's aid. Soon the castle was under siege, not by the Parliamentarians but by the womenfolk of those inside:

> *Presently their wives come to the castle, there they weepe, and wring their hands, and with clamorous oratory persuade their husbands to come home, and not by saving others to expose their owne houses to spoyle and ruine.*

Unwilling to allow such distress to be caused to her tenants, Lady Bankes was forced to agree to the demands of the Parliamentarians and hand over the four guns in exchange for their departure.

However if the Roundheads believed that they had got the better of this determined woman, they were very much mistaken. Thinking that Corfe was no longer a threat they relaxed their vigilance, with the result that Lady Bankes was able to reinforce the castle, obtain provisions and bring in considerable supplies of powder and match. She was also able to request assistance from the Marquis of Hertford, whose Royalist army was 25 miles away near Blandford. Hertford detached Captain Robert Lawrence, a local Royalist, who arrived at the castle with a troop of horse and orders to oversee the castle's defence. He was soon called into action. In mid-June a body of about 200–300 Parliamentarians arrived in Corfe and bombarded the castle from the surrounding hills. When their summons to the castle to surrender was refused they withdrew, but not before burning four houses in the town. On 23 June they were back, this time with a force of 500 men under Sir Walter Erle, MP for Weymouth and Melcombe Regis, who on 2 May had been appointed commander of all Parliament's forces in Dorset.

By now in his mid-fifties, Erle was a member of one of Dorset's leading families and a prominent Puritan. He had first sat in Parliament in 1616 and had a long history of opposition to Royal policies. During Parliament's impeachment of the king's chief minister, the Earl of Strafford, in 1641, his role had been to accuse Strafford of planning to bring an army over from Ireland to subjugate England. However, when pressed to back up the charge with witnesses he is said to have become 'very blank and out of countenance'. Erle, who in 1630 had briefly seen some military service in the Low Countries, seems to have rather fancied himself as a general. He had constructed model redoubts and fortifications in his garden and the walls of his house were festooned with plans of sieges and battles. Supported by Sir Thomas Trenchard, another Dorset Puritan, he had quickly secured Dorchester, Lyme, Weymouth, Wareham and Poole for the Parliamentarian cause and arranged the surrender of Portland Castle. *Mercurius Rusticus* reported that Erle's men:

> ... *brought with them to the siege a demi-canon, a culverin, and two sakers; with these and their small shot they played on the castle on all quarters of it... making their battery strongest where they thought the castle weakest.*

When King Stephen laid siege to Corfe in 1138 and 1139, he had built a large figure-of-eight ringwork about 440yd to the south-west of the castle. Known as 'the Rings', this earthwork still survives today and is generally thought to be where the Parliamentarians sited the bulk of their artillery, although *Mercurius Rusticus* claims that they also placed guns in St Edward's churchyard. Both were within range of the main gate of the castle and when archaeological excavations were carried out there in the 1990s the items recovered included two 32lb balls from a demi-cannon, presumably the one mentioned by *Mercurius Rusticus*. While his guns, some of which had been brought by ship from Portsmouth, bombarded the castle, Erle tried other tactics. Accounts still survive of the expenditure of £2 3s 4d on the construction of the 'boar' and the 'sow', two-wheeled sheds made with boards lined with wool, which were designed to provide cover for the attackers as they approached the castle. They were not a success. According to *Mercurius Rusticus*:

> *the first that moved forward was the sow, but not being musket proof she cast nine of eleven of her farrow; for the musketeers from this castle were so good marksmen at their legs, the only part of all their bodies left without defence, that nine ran away as well as their broken and battered legs would give them leave, and of the two which knew neither how to run away nor well to stay for fear, one was slain.*

The fact that Walter Erle, for all his military pretensions, was being defied by a woman was not lost on the Royalist propagandists. *Mercurius Rusticus* which, predictably, had a somewhat less than complimentary view of Erle's powers of leadership, gleefully claimed that:

> *Sir Walter and the commanders were earnest to press forward the soldiers but as prodigal as they were with the blood of the common soldiers, they were sparing enough of their own… Sir Walter never willingly exposed himself to any hazard, for being by chance endangered with a bullet-shot through his coat afterwards put on a bear's skin… he was seen to creep about on all fours on the sides of the hill to keep himself from danger.*

At some stage the Earl of Warwick, the commander of the Parliamentarian fleet, had sent Erle 150 sailors to help with the siege, together with several cart-loads of petards and other explosive devices, and a number of scaling ladders. Following the failure of his siege engines, Erle resolved to use the ladders in a direct assault upon the castle. To encourage his men he offered large financial rewards to the storming party, promising £20 to the first man to scale the walls, £19 to the next, and so on down to the twentieth. When his assault troops, some of whom were condemned prisoners released specifically for the purpose, seemed distinctly unenthusiastic at the prospect of exposing themselves in such a manner, Erle and his officers decided that a liberal dose of Dutch courage was in order:

...when they found that persuasion could not prevail with such abject low spirited men, the commanders resolve on another course, which was to make them drunk, knowing that drunkenness makes some men fight like lions, that being sober would run away like hares.

After spending £1 12s on 'a firkin of hot waters' for his troops, Erle divided what the Royalists described as his 'pot valiant' (drunken) troops into two parties. While the first attacked the middle ward of the castle which was defended by Captain Lawrence and the bulk of the garrison, the second tried to climb into the upper ward, held by Lady Bankes, her daughters, servants and a handful of soldiers. But as this second group attempted to set their ladders up against the castle walls they were driven back by a barrage of stones and red-hot embers dropped from above by Lady Bankes and her followers. The first party had also failed to make any progress and the attack collapsed. A Parliamentarian writer, who evidently did not share *Mercurius Rusticus*'s low opinion of Erle's courage, observed that:

Such was the baseness and cowardice of the seamen and landmen both that scarce one man of five came on... Sir Walter Erle at first used all the arguments he could to persuade them, but those not prevailing he offered to lead them on himself if they would promise to follow, which they did; but before he was advanced 30 or 40 paces, the bullets coming thick about their ears, they shamefully ran away and left him alone to make a shameful retreat.

Demoralised by the failure of their assault and alarmed by news that the Royalists, who on 13 July had defeated Sir William Waller outside Devizes in Wiltshire, were advancing towards Purbeck, the Parliamentarians lifted the siege. Departing in haste, they left behind their artillery, ammunition and a hundred horses. According to the Royalists, Erle had lost 100 men during the six-week siege – the garrison only two. Shortly afterwards Sir John Bankes, who was conducting judicial affairs in Salisbury, took the opportunity to visit his family in Corfe. It was the last time he would see them. In January 1644 he rejoined the king in Oxford and in December that year he died. He is buried in Christ Church Cathedral.

In 1645, as the tide began to turn against the Royalist cause, Corfe came under renewed pressure. In May the Parliamentarian Committee for the

Western Counties ordered Sir Anthony Ashley Cooper to tighten the block-ade around Corfe. The following month Colonel Robert Butler, the governor of Wareham, staged a surprise raid on the castle and carried away the garrison's herd of cattle. After Parliament's crushing victory at Naseby in July, Royalist strongholds throughout the south and west fell like ninepins and when Sherborne was stormed in August the only Royalist garrisons left in Dorset were Portland and Corfe.

In October 1645 Colonel John Bingham, the Parliamentarian governor of Poole, was ordered to recommence operations against Corfe. Two regiments of foot were placed under his command for the purpose and more reinforce-ments were sent to him in December. However, on 29 January a troop of 120 Royalist horse under a Colonel Cromwell rode from Oxford wearing Parliamentarian scarfs and succeeded in bluffing their way into Wareham, where they captured its governor, Colonel Butler, before riding on to Corfe. It seems that their plan had been to escort Lady Bankes and her entourage to the relative safety of Oxford but the redoubtable lady declined to leave her home. Cromwell handed Butler over to the Corfe garrison and headed back to Oxford only to be ambushed and captured on the way. With the war now obviously lost not all the defenders of Corfe shared the resolution of its owner. Even Captain Lawrence, who had so distinguished himself during the siege of 1643, seems to have had enough. He came to an agreement with Butler and the pair of them escaped.

Soon after, Lieutenant-Colonel Richard Pittman, one of the officers who had accompanied Cromwell on his January raid and who had remained behind in Corfe, approached the castle's new governor, William Anketel, with a sugges-tion. Pittman offered to leave Corfe to fetch one hundred reinforcements from Somerset. The governor agreed to the plan, but what he did not know was that Pittman had secretly contacted the Roundheads and agreed to deliver them the castle in return for a payment of £200, an amnesty and a commission to raise a regiment for Ireland. On leaving Corfe Pittman gathered together a picked force of up to 200 men from the Parliamentarian garrisons of Weymouth and Lulworth before returning to the castle in the early hours of 27 February. Led by Pittman, the Roundheads made their way to a sally-port in the north-east corner of the castle where Anketel was waiting for them. As Pittman's men filed in to the castle the governor must have smelled a rat, for he suddenly ordered the gate to be closed. But it was too late. At least 50 of the Parliamentarians had already entered and, with the bulk of the defenders down in the outer bailey, the intruders rapidly secured the upper wards of the castle. One contemporary account relates that:

> *...the besieged, as soon as the fraud was discovered, fired and threw down great stones upon these intruders* [perhaps from the keep], *but they maintained their post. There were in fact only 6 men of the garrison in the upper part of the castle, for that was considered impregnable. The remainder of the defending force was placed in the lower wards, which had hitherto been the posts of danger.*

At daybreak the defenders, trapped between the interlopers and the besiegers, could see what a hopeless situation they were in. As the Parliamentarians outside the castle began to advance, Anketel had no choice but to call for a parley and accept the terms of surrender he was offered. Despite an awkward moment when two of the besiegers, keen to start plundering, climbed the castle walls and were fired on by the garrison, the Roundheads' final victory had been almost bloodless. According to the Parliamentarians, the besiegers lost 11 men in the 48-day siege, freed 30 of their own comrades who were being held in the castle, and took 140 prisoners (though the local men in the castle were later allowed to slip quietly home). Lady Bankes and her family were permitted to depart in safety though they were obliged to leave their possessions behind. Corfe was then thoroughly looted with the result that many of its fine furnishings ended up in the homes of the victorious Parliamentarian leaders. News of Corfe's capture was quickly conveyed to Westminster and a brief note in the Commons Journal for 5 March 1646 states that, immediately after morning prayers, the House voted for the demolition of the castle. A Captain Hughes of Lulworth was appointed to oversee the work, which involved the explosion of mines under the castle walls. Archaeological excavations have uncovered the trenches dug for the slighting of the outer gatehouse while a cavity dug by the sappers who were trying to demolish the keep can still be seen in its outer wall. Although the work cost over £300 it was only partially successful, leaving the spectacular ruins that can be seen today.

In 1647, following the payment of substantial fines, Mary Bankes recovered her confiscated estates. As the *Dictionary of National Biography* puts it 'In her financial dealings she displayed the same persistence and adroitness demonstrated in her defence of Corfe.' She fought hard to track down her looted property and sought to minimise the fines she paid for her gallant support of the Royalist cause. She lived to see the Restoration of the monarchy, but died in April 1661.

chapter thirteen

The Weaker Vessel?

T he English Civil War was by no means the first occasion in which women defended castles in the absence of their husbands. Medieval women were generally regarded, by males at least, as inferior beings – frail creatures who needed protection and who might influence their menfolk but never command them. Women were excluded from many aspects of public life and, once married, had fewer property rights. On the other hand widows and obedient married women who were able to act independently – in a 'manful' manner – were usually regarded with admiration. One of the most manful of medieval women was Nicola de la Haye, the hereditary castellan or constable of Lincoln Castle and a long-standing ally of King John. She had already defended the castle for 40 days against King Richard's Justiciar, William Longchamp, in 1191 and had been heavily fined by Richard on his return to England. She was to remain loyal to King John throughout his troubled reign. When John visited Lincoln in 1216 Nicola, who by now was widowed and in her late sixties, offered the keys of the castle to the king, saying she was too old to continue as constable. In fact this may well have been little more than a symbolic demonstration of her loyalty to the king and one cannot help suspecting that she would have been rather disgruntled had John taken her offer at face value. In any event John, who needed all the allies he could get, did no such thing. Urging her to remain in charge, he bolstered the formidable old lady's position by appointing her sheriff of the county. It was to prove a wise decision. After John's death in October 1216 Nicola saw off a detachment of the French army which had attempted to seize the castle, and when the French returned the following April she once again took command, holding the castle until 20 May when the besiegers were routed by a force loyal to John's young successor, King Henry III.

In 1399 Sir John Pelham, the constable of Pevensey Castle, left his wife Joan in charge at home when he joined Henry Bolingbroke to support him in his bid to usurp the throne from Richard II. In his absence the castle was besieged by local levies who were loyal to Richard, but Joan kept them at bay. In one of the earliest known letters written by a woman in English, she wrote to her husband to inform him of the situation and to ask for help.

> My dear Lord it is right that you know of my position, I am here laid in a manner of a siege... so that I may not out, nor no vitals get in without much difficulty. Wherefore my dear may it please you, by the advice of your wise council, to give remedy to the salvation of your castle and the malice of your enemies. The Holy Trinity keep you from your enemies and soon send me good tidings of you.
>
> Written at Pevensey in the Castle by your own poor J Pelham

During the English Civil War huge numbers of women found themselves caught up in the fighting, often because the towns and castles in which they lived or worked came under siege. Many women who could have avoided the danger chose to remain with their menfolk. Sir Hugh Cholmley, the governor of Scarborough Castle, recalled that his 'dear wife endured much hardship, yet in the greatest danger would not be daunted but showed a courage even above her sex', and thousands of ordinary women across the nation must have done the same. Inevitably, though, most attention was given to high-born women like Mary Bankes of Corfe, who defended their homes in the absence of their husbands, partly because it was such an unusual occurrence, partly because the women in question did show remarkable qualities of ingenuity, bravery and endurance, and partly because they provided such good copy for propagandists seeking to belittle an enemy by pointing out that he had been defied by a 'weak and feeble' woman.

On 28 August 1642, only six days after King Charles I had raised his standard at Nottingham, his son Prince Rupert with 18 troops of horse raided Caldecote Hall, the Warwickshire home of William Purefoy, a veteran opponent of the king. Purefoy had already left to join Lord Brooke, the local Parliamentarian leader, but in his absence his wife Joan, together with her son-in-law, three maids and eight servants, held off Rupert's men for nearly 12 hours, only surrendering when the Royalists smoked them out by setting fire to some outbuildings. Despite the fact that the tiny garrison is thought to have slain 18 of the attackers, Rupert spared their lives and is said to have been so impressed by their gallant resistance that he refused to allow his men to sack the house.

One woman who found herself reluctantly thrust into the limelight was the remarkable Brilliana Harley of Brampton Bryan in Herefordshire. Her husband, Robert, was a dedicated Puritan and an opponent of Charles I. When war broke out he remained in Westminster leaving his wife at the family home which, unfortunately for Brilliana, was in the middle of one of the most ardently Royalist parts of the country.

Brilliana Harley was a prolific writer and the letters she sent to both her husband and her son Edward, a cavalry officer in Sir William Waller's army, give a detailed and often moving account of how Brilliana was gradually forced into the conflict by the hostile actions of her Royalist neighbours. They also reveal the thoughts and religious views of a courageous woman who missed her husband, worried about her son and felt vulnerable and isolated in Royalist Herefordshire.

Even before the war began there was tension in the area. Lady Harley described how

at Ludlow they set up a maypole, and a thing like a head upon it, and so they did at Croft, and gathered a great many about it, and shot at it in derision of Roundheads...

Known Parliamentarian supporters were roundly abused and intimidated:

Every Thursday some of Ludlow, as they go through the town (of Brampton) *wish all the Puritans hanged and as I was walking one day in the garden, Mr Longly and one of the maids being with me, they looked upon me and wished all the Puritans and Roundheads at Brampton hanged, and when they were gone a little further they cursed you and all your children...*

In many respects, however, Brilliana Harley's early experiences of civil war were similar to those of Mary Bankes at Corfe. For several months after the fighting broke out the local Royalist gentry refrained from directly attacking Brampton. Many, like Sir William Croft of nearby Croft Castle, knew the

Harleys socially and felt that, as the castle represented no great military threat, there was no need to cause a scene. Brampton could be brought to heel by starving it of supplies. The Harleys' cattle were rounded up and seized and the Royalist Sheriff of Hereford ordered all the Harley tenants to pay their rents directly to him. Although there were sporadic attacks on the Harley estate and some of Brilliana's servants and supporters were assaulted or jailed, the castle was largely left alone. All this was to change at the end of July 1643 when Sir William Vavasour was appointed Royalist commander in the area. A professional soldier from Yorkshire, Vavasour had no qualms about commencing operations against Brampton and surrounded the castle with a force of some 700 men. However, when Vavasour summoned Brilliana Harley to surrender Brampton Bryan she cannily replied that she could not possibly do so without her absent husband's permission. With 50 musketeers she successfully defended the castle and the 50 civilians within it for seven weeks. Captain Priamus Davies, who served under her during the siege, later wrote that she led the defence

with such a masculine bravery, both for religion, resolution, wisdom and warlike policy, that her equal I never yet saw...

During the second half of the siege the Royalists were under the command of Sir Henry Lingen, who was later to earn fame as the defender of Goodrich. Even at this stage, however, Lingen seems to have made no attempt to storm the place. Instead, cheered on by crowds of spectators who had gathered on the surrounding hills to watch the show, he bombarded the castle with his guns, siting some of them in a churchyard less than a hundred yards from its walls. According to Captain Davies, Lingen's men also peppered the defenders with insults,

calling us Essex's bastards, Waller's bastards. Harley's bastards, rogues, traitors, thieves, traitors...their rotten poisoned language annoyed us more than their poisoned bullets.

After Lingen abandoned the siege in early September, following the Royalists' failure to capture Gloucester, Brilliana Harley took the opportunity to hit back at her enemies. Her men plundered Royalist property in order to restock the castle with supplies and she even ordered a raid across the Welsh border. By this time, however, Brilliana was exhausted. Her health broke down and at the end of October she died of pneumonia. Charles I who, like all his supporters, had revelled in the exploits of Mary Bankes, dismissed Brilliana Harley's brave resistance as the result of bad advice on the part of unscrupulous men who had taken advantage of a woman's 'weaker nature'. In April 1644 Brampton surrendered to the Royalists and was burned to the ground.

With her Royalist husband absent on the Isle of Man, it fell to Charlotte de la Tremouille, Countess of Derby, to defend the Stanley family seat at Lathom House against the Parliamentarian force that arrived there at the end of February 1644. When the countess refused to surrender, the Parliamentarians surrounded the house with earthworks and began an intensive bombardment with their artillery, including a demi-cannon and a large mortar. Although the garrison launched two successful sorties, they were unable to silence the mortar. Despite the efforts of the countess, who calmly carried on with her embroidery as the great stones it fired came crashing down into the house, the morale of the garrison began to waver. On 23 April, confident of victory, Parliamentarian commander Colonel Alexander Rigby sent a drummer forward with terms of surrender. He had even invited his friends and neighbours along to watch the show. But the countess was having none of it. She loudly told the drummer that 'a due reward for thy pains would be to hang thee at my gate, but thou art only the foolish instrument of a traitor's pride...' and sent him back with the message that she and her children would rather die in the flames of the house than surrender it. Inspired by their lady's words, the listening garrison vowed to fight on and two days later a party of them sallied out of Lathom's east gate, captured the mortar and dragged it back into the house in triumph. A month later, hearing that Prince Rupert and her husband were marching to the countess's relief, the Parliamentarians abandoned the siege.

Many other ordinary women, whose names have not been recorded, also played an active part in siege warfare. In April 1644 Sir Michael Woodhouse, who had resumed operations against Brampton Bryan, wrote to Prince Rupert about a woman he had captured:

I have taken a woman that was sent out of the castle with a letter to a man of this county for relief from Gloucester. The man I have likewise... the queen was returning in man's apparel and offered [pretended] to be a soldier in Croft's company. I desire your Highness's pleasure concerning them...

In this context a 'queen' was a derogatory term for a young woman. Clearly, the hard-pressed defenders of Brampton were hoping for help from Gloucester, the nearest Parliamentarian city of any note. Gloucester itself had withstood a major Royalist siege in 1643 when a quick-thinking woman is reported to have extinguished a large mortar bomb that had been fired into the city, by pouring a bucket of water over it. During the siege of Worcester local women repaired the city's defences, often under fire. Women also took an active part in the defence of the Parliamentarian town of Lyme, putting out fires and reloading muskets for their menfolk. When the siege was eventually lifted they rushed out with picks and spades and levelled the abandoned Royalist earthworks in three days. Writing in October 1645 during the siege of Chester a member of the Royalist garrison noted that

by this time our women are all on fire, striving through a gallant emulation to outdo our men and will make good our yielding walls or lose their lives. Seven are shot and three slain, yet they scorn to leave their undertaking and thus they continue for ten days space.

Other women took part in the fighting itself. Female snipers are reputed to have fired at the Royalists during the storming of Leicester in May 1645 and it is said that during the siege of Bridgwater in July 1645 the governor's wife, Lady Wyndham, even took a potshot at Oliver Cromwell. But for sheer unbridled ferocity, Elizabeth Dowdall of Kilfinny stood head and shoulders above the rest. She was married to Sir Hardress Waller, himself a soldier of some repute who was later to sign the death warrant of King Charles I, and seems to have taken to war like a duck to water. In 1641, soon after the outbreak of the Irish rebellion, she raised a company of soldiers and when a group of rebels tried to plunder her fortified house she seized their horses and had ten of the men hanged. More rebels surrounded the house only to die horribly when Lady Dowdall sent out soldiers with grenades to set fire to their quarters. Eventually Richard Stephenson, a leading rebel, arrived on the scene with 3,000 men and two 'sows' – wheeled shelters with pitched roofs to provide cover for his troops as they advanced. It is with barely disguised relish that the fearsome Lady Dowdall describes what happened next.

The ninth of January, the High Sheriff of the county, and all the power of the county, came with three thousand men to besiege me. They brought two sows and thirty scaling-ladders against me. They wrote many attempting letters to me to yield to them which I answered with contempt and scorn. They were three weeks and four days besieging me before they could bring these sows to me, being building of them all that time upon my own land, yet every day and night in fight with me. The Thursday before Ash Wednesday High-Sheriff, Richard Stephenson, came up in the front of the army with his drums and pipers, but I sent him a shot in the head that made him bid the world goodbye, and routed the whole army, we shot so hot... On Thursday they drew their sows nearer, and Friday they came on at night with a full career and a great acclamation of joy, even hard to the castle. But I sent such a free welcome to them that turned their mirth into moaning. I shot iron bullets that pierced through their sows, though they were lined with iron gridds and flock-beds and bolsters, so that I killed their pigs and by the enemy's confession that night two hundred of their men.

chapter fourteen

Goodrich 1646

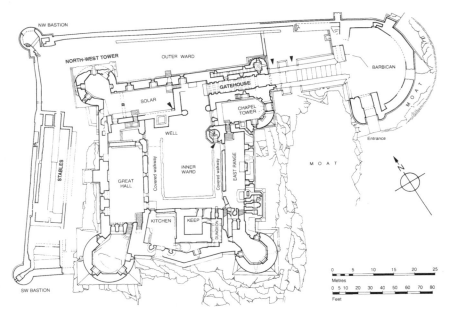

Goodrich Castle

Built largely of red sandstone and protected by a deep cutting into the rock on which it stands, Goodrich Castle overlooks an ancient and much-used crossing of the River Wye. Its medieval owners included some of England's great noble warriors: Richard de Clare, William Marshal, Aymer de Valence and John Talbot. Even so Goodrich's history was generally peaceful until the outbreak of the Civil War. Although Herefordshire as a whole was largely Royalist in sympathies, Goodrich's owner at that time was the Parliamentarian Earl of Kent. As a result, the castle was briefly held for Parliament by a local Roundhead, Colonel Robert Kyrle from nearby Walford Court. However, Herefordshire was largely secured for the king in 1643, the castle passed into Royalist hands and a garrison was established there towards the end of the year. By mid-1645 the war had turned decisively in Parliament's favour and, when Colonel John Birch captured Hereford in December, Goodrich was left as the centre of Royalist resistance in the area.

Much of what we know about John Birch's military service is derived from an extraordinary biography written in the second person by one of his subordinates, a man named Roe. It is tempting to speculate that Roe, who was possibly Birch's secretary, may have exaggerated some of the martial exploits of his superior. But if even only half of what he has written is true, it is difficult to escape the conclusion that John Birch was one of Parliament's most courageous and resourceful soldiers.

Birch was born in 1615 at Ardwick near Manchester into a family of prominent Presbyterians. In 1633 he moved to Bristol where he set up as a merchant and married Alice Selfe, the widow of a rich grocer. At the outbreak of the Civil War Birch supported Parliament and served as a captain in the Bristol Militia. He helped foil a Royalist conspiracy to seize the city in March 1643 but when Bristol fell to Prince Rupert in July, Birch sold up his business and moved to London. There he met the Parliamentarian leader Sir Arthur Hesilrige who appointed him Lieutenant-Colonel of his regiment of foot, bound for service with Sir William Waller in the south of England. Birch soon made a name for himself, leading the assault upon St Lawrence churchyard during Waller's victory at Alton. The following January he was severely wounded by a shot in the stomach during the attack on Arundel Castle. According to Roe, Birch held in his 'gutts', stopping the hole with his finger and hiding the wound from his men before eventually collapsing. Giving him up for dead, Waller's surgeons did not even bother to dress the wound but it seems that the severe cold helped congeal the blood and Birch miraculously survived.

By March he had recovered sufficiently to fight at Cheriton and in July he distinguished himself at Cropredy Bridge. In September he took command of a Kentish regiment of foot and helped to defend Plymouth which was under severe pressure following the Earl of Essex's defeat at Lostwithiel. During the fighting there he took one of the Arundel family prisoner and, according to Roe, wore the captured Royalist's sword for the rest of his military career. In late October 1644 Birch fought with his regiment at the second battle of Newbury and took a leading role in the pursuit of the retreating Royalists. Birch's regiment was not incorporated into Parliament's New Model Army, formed in February 1645, but was later attached to it and in September Birch took part in the recapture of his old home town, Bristol, leading the storm of the city's Harnell Gate. Birch then briefly served as governor of the city but in early December he was ordered by Parliament's Committee of Safety:

> to draw out 1,000 foot and your own horse and march to Herefordshire; and to endeavour…to distress the city of Hereford, and use all means to take it in.

Hereford had already seen off a Scottish siege earlier in the year but on 18 December, joined by Colonel Thomas Morgan from Gloucester and assisted by some disaffected elements inside the walls, Birch launched a surprise attack on its Byster Gate and soon the city was in Parliamentarian hands. It has been argued that Birch's part in the capture of Hereford was a comparatively minor one and that war weariness and dissension among the defenders may have been more important, but Parliament was in no doubt where the credit should go. On 22 December it publicly thanked Birch, voted £60,000 to pay his men and appointed him governor of the city. In many ways this was something of a poisoned chalice, for both Hereford and the surrounding area remained strongly Royalist in sympathies, but the appointment was accompanied by an annuity of £50. This was to be paid to Birch from the estate of the man who was to cause him more trouble than anyone else over the next few months – Sir Henry Lingen.

If anyone fitted the popular image of the reckless, dashing Cavalier, it was Henry Lingen. A prominent Herefordshire Royalist, the Catholic Lingen had been sheriff of the county in 1637–8 and had also served as a captain in the Herefordshire Trained Bands. At the outbreak of the Civil War the king appointed him one of the county's commissioners of array, tasked with raising troops for the royal army, an activity he seems to have carried out with some success. He was captured in March 1643 when Lord Herbert's Royalist army was overrun by Sir William Waller at Hignham, but was soon exchanged for a Parliamentarian prisoner and was reinstalled as sheriff. Later that year he took over from Sir William Vavasour at the siege of the isolated Parliamentarian stronghold of Brampton Bryan, which was defended by Lady Brilliana Harley in the absence of her husband Robert, the prominent Parliamentarian MP.

Lingen abandoned the siege following the Royalists' failure to capture Gloucester but Brilliana Harley died soon after, exhausted by her exertions, and in April 1644 Brampton was surrendered to Sir Michael Woodhouse and was burned to the ground. That year the king's nephew, Prince Rupert, reorganised the military administration of the Welsh Marches and appointed Lingen governor of Goodrich Castle. Knighted by Charles I in 1645, Lingen was in Hereford when it fell to the Parliamentarians that December but managed to escape across the frozen River Wye and made his way back to Goodrich.

By now it must have been abundantly clear to even the most optimistic Cavalier that, militarily at least, the Royalist cause was lost, but Lingen refused to give up hope. Strengthening the castle's defences, he gathered together a garrison of about 200 diehard Royalists, later described by one Parliamentarian as 'a nest of Papists and rigid Malignants'. The majority seem to have been locals who knew the surrounding area well and they used this knowledge to good effect, raiding almost at will and making life thoroughly difficult for the Roundheads. On 5 March 1646 Birch was ordered to draw out troops from his garrison at Hereford and join with a force under Colonel Thomas Morgan and Sir William Brereton, to intercept Sir Jacob Astley who was planning to march to Oxford to join the king with what was in effect the last remaining Royalist army. But Birch realised that to leave Hereford would have left the city and surrounding area dangerously exposed to raids from Goodrich. As Roe put it:

> ...this could not be done without utter ruin to the country, except you could some way break and destroy the forces under Sir Henry Lingen; but especially the horse, who undoubtedly when you were gone so far would bring all the country to subjection and come up to the gates of Hereford itself.

In a letter to the Speaker of the Commons, Birch concurred with this view, writing that the Goodrich garrison was:

> so active that a passenger could not be safe between Gloucester and Hereford, nor could I quarter horse abroad but they were in much danger, nor could I draw forth towards Ludlow or Worcester but they would come near unto the city to plunder...

Faced with this awkward situation, Birch came up with a daring plan. If he was not yet in a position to capture Goodrich Castle he could at least reduce the garrison's capacity to carry out raids by depriving them of their horses. With Colonel Kyrle, who had briefly held Goodrich for Parliament, in his entourage, Birch would have had detailed information about the layout of the castle and the height of its walls. Crucially, he would also have known the location of Goodrich's stables, which were in the outer ward of the castle, built against its lower outer wall. On 9 March the weather was miserable and Birch sensed an opportunity. Knowing that Lingen's horses would be shut up in their stables for the night he set off from Hereford with 500 horse and foot and marched in great secrecy to Goodrich, arriving there just before dawn. While the bulk of his force created a noisy diversion in front of the castle's main gate, 100 musketeers armed with firelocks used ladders to scale its outer wall near the stables. Roe relates that:

> ...the castle itself, hearing so great a noise about the gate, supposed the danger there, therefore applied all their force thither. In the meantime the stable was entered, a hole beaten through the back of the wall according to order and then led out by the party 76 horse: 12 were left that would not come out; whereupon instantly that great stable, being full of hay, straw and combustible matter, was fired and burned to the ground, with the horse, saddles and all things else for the enemy's use.

Meanwhile, according to Birch, another party of his men:

> ...fell on their out-guard, in a place called the Boat-House [presumably guarding the crossing over the Wye], which was within pistol shot of the castle which held out 2 hours until it was digged through; then they desired quarter for their lives.

Returning to Hereford with 17 prisoners and as many horses as his men could round up, Birch now felt secure enough to march to join Morgan against Astley and on 21 March, in what was to be the last pitched battle of the First Civil War, the Royalists were overwhelmed at Stow-on-the-Wold. Astley's men seem to have put up a stiff resistance and Birch's troops lost 33 horses, including the one Birch himself was riding. However, if the Parliamentarian leader thought he had put a stop to Lingen's activities he was mistaken. While Birch was away campaigning Lingen, who had managed to replace at least some of his lost horses, made a daring bid to recapture Hereford. Attacking in broad daylight with only 30 horse he charged the city's southern gate, in the hope that the traditionally Royalist inhabitants of Hereford would rise up and join him. However, no such rising took place and Lingen was eventually driven off – but not before he had killed four guards and thoroughly alarmed the garrison.

As the Royalist cause crumbled throughout Britain, Birch spent the early spring mopping up the last pockets of resistance in his area, and at the end of May he turned his attention to Goodrich. In a letter delivered to Lingen on 13 June Birch informed him of the impending surrender of the Royalist capital, Oxford, and urged him to deliver up Goodrich as well:

> *... I must let you know that Oxford is to be delivered up the 19th instant... I have been studious of your welfare, which to advance I find no visible way left, but that you submit unto the pleasure of the High Court of Parliament; in whose name and for whose use I demand of you the possession of this castle of Goodrich... And for those gentlemen now under your protection, if they shall put themselves under mine, I shall not deceive them of that civility which they may expect; and shall thankfully acknowledge the goodness of Almighty God in sparing a further effusion of blood: it being my desire hereby to declare unto you my especial care to prevent... But that you shall persist to a further enraging of those under my command... and blood and utter ruin follow, I hereby desire to be excused...*
> *Your real friend, John Birch, June 13 1646*

For all its social niceties, Birch's message was clear – surrender while you still have the chance or face the consequences if my troops, who are itching for a fight, are forced to storm your castle. Militarily, there was no reason whatsoever why Lingen should fight on. There was no prospect of relief and even the king himself had surrendered – to the Scots at Newark on 5 May. But fight on he did. The following day one of Lingen's drummers brought Birch an equally polite reply:

> *Sir, I received yesterday a summons from you, wherein you demand of me this castle to be delivered unto your hands for the use of the parliament. The King placed me in it, by his commission, to keep it for him and for his use and, until I shall receive an immediate order or command from him to the contrary, I shall do it to the uttermost of my power...*
> *Your loving friend, Henry Lingen*

Now the gloves were off. Birch replied:

Sir, I have received your resolution by your drummer, which far better contents those under my command than myself, who really desired your welfare...

Establishing his headquarters at nearby Walford Court, Birch ordered trenches to be dug near to the castle and commenced operations to undermine its walls, a difficult task given the hardness of the rock on which they were built. Nevertheless Birch's men persevered and as their mine inched its way towards the castle the defenders began digging a countermine of their own in a bid to intercept the Parliamentarians. On 18 June Birch wrote to the Speaker of the House of Commons:

I am approached within the reach of their stones, which they throw abundantly, and am now almost ready to play upon them with a mortar piece, which I have cast here, carrying a shell of above two hundred weight; and have planted my battery and am going on with my mines; for effecting of all which, a considerable quantity of powder will be speedily necessary.
I therefore humbly entreat your honour will be pleased to move the honourable house for eighty barrels, which will much forward the service...

A week later an extract of Birch's letter was read to the Commons who ordered that Birch should receive the powder he needed. The mortar piece to which Birch was referring was, according to Roe, the largest in England at the time. It has been suggested that it may have been cast at the Old Forge, a mile and a half away from the castle, where the Wye meets the Ross–Monmouth Road. Birch himself fired 19 of the 22 granadoes that the great mortar lobbed into the castle and did the job so accurately that he was later able to report that 'I had very much torn the castle with my mortar piece, that no whole room was left in it...'

In addition Birch cut the pipes that brought water into the castle and its stone cisterns were also damaged by the bombardment. Cannon and mortar fire, mining and countermining, continued until 30 July when the north-west tower collapsed under the bombardment, blocking Lingen's countermine and opening up a breach in the castle walls. The way was now open for Birch to storm the castle and he began to deploy his forces for an assault. Seeing this Lingen, who knew he could do no more and wishing to preserve the lives of his garrison, hauled down his colours and hung up a white flag of truce. It seems that Lingen attempted to persuade Birch to grant his men the 'honours of war' – the right to march out of the castle with their arms and ammunition and depart unmolested with drums beating and trumpets playing – but Birch was not prepared to offer such generous terms to men who had caused the Parliamentarians so much trouble and who were now at his mercy. On 31 July he wrote that:

> *...their desires were honourable terms, which I thought not fit to grant, neither to give them any thing beyond mercy for their lives, their persons to be wholly at my dispose; upon which terms I have this day received possession of this castle.*

Tradition has it that the Royalist garrison, of up to 50 officers and 150 men, marched out of the castle and into captivity to a tune known as 'Sir Harry Lingen's fancy'. In fact this seems unlikely: the right of a garrison to march out of a castle to music was one of the 'honours of war' and would be specifically mentioned in a surrender document if it was granted. Other than their lives, Lingen's men were granted nothing.

Lingen was imprisoned in Hereford but was released two months later after offering to compound for his estates (pay a fine based on the value of his property) and promising not to bear arms against Parliament again. Within days he had broken his parole by returning to Hereford wearing his sword and caused a riot by challenging the mayor of the city to a duel. During the Second Civil War of 1648 he raised a troop of horse for the king but after an initial success at Leominster was defeated and captured. Seriously wounded, he was imprisoned in Redd Castle in Montgomeryshire. In November the House of Commons ordered him to be banished from the country but the sentence was revoked the following month. Nevertheless he was heavily fined for his activities in the two wars and in 1651, still owing £1,200, was forced to sell off part of his estates. At the Restoration he was elected MP for Hereford and re-elected the following year, only to die of smallpox in Gloucester on his way home from the first session of Parliament.

Following the capture of Goodrich, Birch took his mortar to the siege of

Raglan Castle and was present at its surrender in August 1646. That December he took his seat in the Commons as one of the members for Leominster. Excluded from Parliament by Pride's Purge – Colonel Thomas Pride's purge of the more moderate Parliamentarian MPs – he opposed the execution of the king and even met with Charles II on the eve of the battle of Worcester in September 1651. His opposition to Cromwell meant that, like Lingen, Birch also spent some time in Hereford Gaol, being imprisoned there for eight months in 1655. In 1659 he played a prominent part in the Restoration and was rewarded by Charles II with the appointment of Auditor of the Excise for life. He died, aged 75, in 1691 and is buried in Weobley Church in Herefordshire beneath a substantial monument.

On 1 March 1647 Parliament ordered the slighting of Goodrich Castle to prevent its possible use as a Royalist base in the future, although much of the job had already been done by Birch's mortar. The castle still belonged to the Dowager Countess of Kent, whose family had supported Parliament during the Civil War, and she was paid £1,000 compensation for the destruction of her property. After the surrender of Raglan Castle Birch brought his great mortar back to Hereford. Known as *Roaring Meg* it occupied a number of locations in the city before being moved to Churchill Gardens Museum. In December 2003 Herefordshire County Council lent it to English Heritage and it can now be seen in the courtyard of Goodrich Castle, the place it did so much to destroy.

chapter fifteen

Pendennis 1646

The Fal estuary with its deep sheltered waters has always been a haven for ships but its isolation has also made it a potential anchorage for an invading fleet. So when Charles V and Francis I formed an alliance against England in 1538, Henry VIII ordered the construction of two forts to defend the estuary, one on the Pendennis headland, the other across the water at St Mawes. Part of a chain of similar coastal forts running from Milford Haven to Hull, the two castles were begun in 1540 and completed in about five years. Both were built with the needs of modern artillery in mind. Pendennis originally consisted of a circular tower with guns on two floors and the roof, but its location high up on the headland meant that it was not able to cover all the approaches to the harbour. A circular gun platform, known as a chemise, was soon added at ground level. St Mawes, which consisted of three stone bastions around a circular keep, was much nearer to sea level which meant it was far better suited to its primary purpose – firing at ships out to sea – but was highly vulnerable to a land attack.

In 1596 it was discovered that a Spanish invasion force had only been prevented from landing in England by high winds off Land's End; it had been planning to seize the Pendennis headland and use it as the bridgehead for an invasion. As a result, the Earl of Essex and Sir Walter Raleigh inspected the defences at Pendennis and recommended extensive, and urgent, improvements. A small fort was built nearer to sea level to increase the effectiveness of the castle's firepower while extensive earth ramparts with angled bastions were dug around the Henrician castle. In 1627 worsening relations with France and Spain led to further improvements by the military engineer Bernard Johnson, who enclosed the remaining high ground of the peninsula within an earthen rampart known as a hornwork and constructed a ravelin – a projecting outwork – on which to mount cannons.

Pendennis and St Mawes were held for the king from the very outset of the Civil War and Falmouth became an important Royalist base for the import of arms and supplies while privateers operated from the harbour, preying on Parliamentarian shipping. On 17 January 1643 the Royalists received an unexpected windfall when three Parliamentarian ships, loaded with arms and money, were driven by a storm into Falmouth harbour where they were seized by the Cavaliers. When the war began the governor of Pendennis was Sir Nicholas Slanning, a committed Royalist and MP for the local town of Penryn. But when Slanning was mortally wounded at the storming of Bristol in July 1643 his place as governor was taken by the veteran Sir John Arundel of Trerice. Arundel, who was at least 70, had been present at Queen Elizabeth's review of her army at Tilbury during the Armada campaign of 1588 and as a result was affectionately known as 'Old Tilbury'. Pendennis was to have its share of significant visitors in the next two years. Queen Henrietta Maria stayed there in July 1644 before sailing for France. In 1644 the Scottish courtier James, Duke of Hamilton, was imprisoned in the castle by the king under suspicion of disloyalty. He remained there until November 1645 when he was moved to St Michael's Mount. In late 1645, with Royalist fortunes on the wane, Lord Hopton and Sir Edward Hyde visited Pendennis to organise the strengthening of the defences of Falmouth, which they saw as a potential landing place for foreign reinforcements. As a result a fort was constructed at the mouth of the Helford River to control the sheltered waters beyond and work was begun on further ramparts and an advanced bastion at Upton's Mount on Pendennis headland.

On 16 February 1646, however, Hopton's Royalist army was decisively defeated by Sir Thomas Fairfax at Torrington in north Devon. As Fairfax's victorious New Model Army advanced into Cornwall, the 15-year-old Prince of Wales, nominal Captain-General of Royalist forces in the West Country, left Pendennis for the Isles of Scilly. When the bulk of Hopton's defeated army surrendered at Truro on 12 March most observers expected Pendennis to follow suit. As a Parliamentarian letter writer stated:

We doubt not, but Pendennis will upon the disbanding of these forces, incline to moderate terms, the Governor thereof is a gentleman of good fortune and estate in the country, and in all likelihood will not be so mad

*as to see all the whole gentry at liberty, enjoying their own, and himself as
it were in prison, enjoying nothing that is his own.*

But stubborn Old Tilbury had other ideas. Reinforced by a few elements of
Hopton's army who had not surrendered, and joined by a large number of
diehard Royalist officers, he resolved to hold Pendennis until relief could arrive
from the continent. One Parliamentarian described the garrison as 'the most
desperate persons, and the violentest enemies that the parliament hath in this
kingdom'. Fairfax's army soon arrived in the area. On 12 March
Parliamentarian troops exposed the vulnerability of St Mawes to a land attack
by taking up positions on the high ground above the castle, and its governor,
Hannibal Bonython, surrendered without a shot being fired. Soon after, the
new fort at Helford also surrendered to the Parliamentarians with the result
that the Royalists lost their control of the Fal estuary. Arundel planned to deny
the Roundheads shelter, by burning Falmouth, and cover, by destroying
Arwenack, a large house that lay within musket range of their outworks. In the
event Falmouth, which was known at the time as Pen-y-cym-Cuick (or
Pennycomequick in English sources), was saved by the arrival of Fairfax's army,
and although the Royalists set fire to Arwenack it was only partially destroyed.
On 18 March Sir Thomas Fairfax summoned Arundel to surrender:

*Sir, Being come into these parts with the army, where it hath pleased God
to give us so good success, as no body of an army is remaining to oppose
us... I thought it fit before any extremity of force were used against you, to
send you this summons, by which I demand you to deliver up the castle of
Pendennis, and all things belonging to that garrison for the service of the
kingdom, which if you incline to, you may have conditions befitting
yourself and the quality of those that are with you: I expect your answer in
two hours, and rest your servant, Thomas Fairfax.*

Arundel's reply was immediate – and predictably defiant:

*Sir, The castle was committed to my government by his Majesty, who by
our laws hath the command of the castles and forts of this kingdom... I
wonder you demand the castle without authority from his Majesty; which
if I should render, I brand myself and my posterity with the indelible
character of treason. And having taken less than two minutes resolution,*

*I resolve that I will here bury myself before I deliver up this castle to such
as fight against his Majesty, and that nothing you can threaten is
formidable to me in respect of the loss of loyalty and conscience.
Your Servant, John Arundel.*

Although there had not been time to complete the earthworks at Upton's
Mount, Pendennis still had formidable defences and could only be approached
along a narrow strip of land from the north. Well stocked with ammunition,
bristling with cannon and with over 1,000 experienced soldiers to defend it,
Pendennis would have been a nightmare to take by storm. But that was never
Fairfax's intention. As a member of his army wrote the following day:

*Questionless the place is very strong, as well by its natural situation (it
being almost an island) as by art and great industry; and it is victualled
(as they say) for nine or ten months, and they have in it about one
thousand or twelve hundred men, all desperate persons and good soldiers;
and they have powder and shot great store, and at least eighty great guns
mounted, besides forty in the ship which lies on the north side of the castle.
Therefore the general resolves to block it up very close both by land and
sea... and for that if we draw a line thwart the narrow neck of land...
Pendennis Castle will remain unto them but as a close and sure prison,
and so in the end the belly will conquer them, without striking a stroke.*

Instead of attempting to storm the castle the Parliamentarians dug in for a
siege, cutting trenches across the headland and building a fort for their cannon
near to Arwenack. Two regiments of foot, Hammond's and Fortescue's, were
billeted in Falmouth and a flotilla of ships under Captain William Batten
completed the blockade. Both sides began a sporadic bombardment, the
Royalists using the guns from a beached warship, the *Great George*, to bolster
their firepower. It took the Parliamentarians three weeks to finish their earthworks and on 26 March a London newspaper reported the death of Lieutenant-
Colonel Oliver Ingoldsby of Colonel Richard Fortescue's regiment, 'who with
other commanders going to view Pendennis Castle received a shot from the
enemy who lay in ambush behind a mud-wall'. At this stage Colonel Robert
Hammond, a veteran of Naseby who was later to become the king's jailor at
Carisbrooke, led the besiegers but when he left the siege to oversee the
reduction of St Michael's Mount, Fortescue took command. It was not long

before the Parliamentarian blockade began to bite. Although the food stocks in the castle may well have lasted the original garrison for eight or nine months, the arrival of the extra troops from Hopton's defeated army put an additional strain on supplies that also had to support over 200 women and children. Matters were not helped in early June by the capture off Pendennis of a Royalist ship loaded with provisions for the castle, and on 30 June *The Perfect Diurnal*, a Parliamentarian newspaper, reported that the Royalists' provisions were 'well near spent'.

By the end of July the defenders, still hoping for relief from France, were reduced to eating horseflesh. About this time one small boat did manage to break through the Parliamentarian blockade, much to the joy of the garrison. The besiegers concluded that it must have been heavily laden with supplies for otherwise it would not have been worth undertaking such a risky venture, but it was later reported that there was little on it 'save a hogshead or two of wine'. By this time sickness had hit the garrison, lack of food was causing dissent and, although the Cavaliers lit fires every night to guide in a relief force, there was no sign of help from abroad. In early August Arundel announced his willingness to discuss terms with Fortescue and Batten. Negotiations initially stalled. According to John Haslock, who was Batten's surgeon, Sir John Digby and a number of other Royalist officers hatched a plan to blow up the castle and everyone in it, friend and foe, if they were not granted honourable terms. Haslock writes that they were only to be prevented from doing so by their own men, though the fact that the surrender terms eventually offered were so generous may have had more to do with it. On 16 August the surrender document was finally signed and on the following day the exhausted defenders marched out, with full honours of war. A Parliamentarian newspaper reported:

...The number of soldiers that marched out were 800, who laid down their arms half a mile from the castle, and disbanded; most of the officers and gentlemen intend to go beyond seas. In the castle was six double barrels of powder, 37 single found presently, more heard of, 1,100 round shot, 2,500 weight of match, 2,000 weight of small shot, 1,900 muskets, 95 pieces of cannon, a murtherer, some pikes and brown bills, 4 knights, 8 colonels, 6 lieut-colonels, 6 majors, 17 captains, 17 lieutenants, 21 ensigns, 3 quartermasters, 15 officers of the train, 16 gunners, the whole number above 1,000. 200 sick left behind, 200 women and children, their provisions remaining little and bad, their spirits and resolutions great and

desperate. A hundred of them resolved, yea engaged themselves by oath, whereof the Lord Digby's brother was one, to blow up the castle and themselves, if they could not get honourable terms, which was grounded upon the dissolving the first treaty.'

Although it seems more likely that the Parliamentarians were generous because they could afford to be (*see* Appendices), the Royalist historian Clarendon writes that, although the garrison had virtually nothing left to eat, they had conducted the surrender negotiations

with such resolution and unconcernedness that the enemy concluded they were in no straits; and so gave them the conditions they proposed; which were as good as any garrison in England had accepted.

Many of the departing garrison were severely ill with starvation and Batten's surgeon found himself left with as many as 400 sick to care for. Sadly, as had happened at Rouen nearly 250 years earlier, many died after eating their first proper meal in months. According to one account:

...the hunger-starved soldiers of Pendennis, who came out thence, regaling too freely on victuals and drink, brought themselves into incurable diseases, whereof many died. So that here, as in many other places, it was observed that more men and women died by too often putting their hands to their mouths, than by clapping their hands to their swords.

Pendennis was the last Royalist garrison in England to yield to the Roundheads. When, two days later, the Marquess of Worcester surrendered Raglan Castle to the Parliamentarians, the First Civil War was effectively at an end. The strategic importance of Pendennis, however, ensured that it avoided being slighted by Parliament's victorious army. It was immediately garrisoned and remained in military use for more than 300 years.

Appendices

I Jordan Fantosme's account of the defence of Wark in 1174

A clerk in the service of Henry of Blois, Bishop of Winchester, Jordan Fantosme wrote a 2,000-line French-verse chronicle of the events of 1173–4 when, in a bid to regain Northumbria, William the Lion of Scotland invaded northern England in support of the rebellion against Henry II. Fantosme appears to have been well acquainted with many of the events he recorded and specifically says that he was present at the capture of William the Lion outside Alnwick, claiming 'I do not relate a fable, as one who has heard say, but as one who was there, and I myself saw it'. In this extract, translated into English in the 1850s, Fantosme describes William's unsuccessful attempt in 1174 to capture the important border fortress of Wark, which was defended by Roger d'Estuteville, a loyal supporter of Henry II. This account of the siege is often referred to for its description of the disastrous performance of William's siege engine, but it seems clear that for Fantosme the key factor in the Scottish failure to take Wark was the leadership of d'Estuteville, who is portrayed throughout the poem as a God-fearing and inspirational leader.

> *Then sent the king of Scotland for his knights,*
> *The earls of his land, all the best warriors;*
> *To Wark he wished to lay siege by his good counsellors,*
> *He wished to have the castle by Flemings and archers,*
> *By good stone-bows, by his engines very strong*
> *And by his slingers and his cross-bowmen.*
> *Will you hear of Roger how he behaved himself?*
> *He was not the least dismayed when this host came to him:*
> *He had in his train knights more than twenty,*
> *Certainly, the best serjeants that ever baron retained,*
> *The host was marvellous, of great chivalry,*
> *Of Flemings and Border-men fierce was the company.*
> *Roger d'Estuteville has garrisoned his house,*
> *He does not fear their siege the value of a clove of garlic:*
> *He has a very gentle baronage to whom he trusts much,*
> *And to exhort them well he did not forget.*
> *By a Monday morning were equipped*
> *Those who shall assault the castle, Flemings they were named,*
> *Then you might see bucklers seized and shields buckled on,*

The portcullis assaulted, as you may soon hear,
By wonderful daring they came to the ditches;
Those who were inside did not forget themselves;
They soon struck each other and were so mingled together
That I never saw a better defence in these two kingdoms.
The Flemings were very daring and courageous,
And the others much enraged in their fortress.
Soon you might see serjeants and Flemings so mingled,
Shields and bucklers broken, pennons displayed,
Flemings turning back from the portcullises, wounded;
Some were carried from the portcullises by others;
Never will they cry Arras! Dead they are and buried.
Long lasted this assault but little succeeded…
Roger d'Estuteville exhorted his men…
'Shoot not your arrows forth but on great occasions…
Spare your arms, I say that to you, archers;
But when you see need and great complete assaults,
Then defend your heads like gentle chevaliers..'
…And the king of Scotland was greatly enraged.
When he saw his serjeants die and often fall
And saw that he was not gaining ground he was grieved in heart;
And said to his knights in his great irritation:
'make your stone-bow come hastily;
It will soon break the gate, if the engineer lies not;
And we shall take the outer fortification with no delay.'
Hear, lords, of the stone-bow how it went on:
The first stone which it ever cast at them,
The stone was scarcely parted from the sling
When it knocked one of their knights to the ground.
Were it not for his armour and the shield which he had,
To none of his lineage had he ever returned;
Much must he hate the engineer who contrived that for them…
When the stone-bow failed him [William] ordered up the other:
He fain would burn the castle, he knows not what to do better;
But Jesus the glorious, the Creator of all things,
Turned against the king of Scotland the wind very contrary,
And to Roger the baron it began much to please.

Now he has such gladness, in his life he never had more.
Then said King William: 'Let us raise this siege;
I see my people destroyed and the mischief which cuts us off.
Certainly this affair grieves me much at heart.
Roger d'Estuteville has found us out.'

II Roger of Wendover's account of the siege of Bedford, 1224

In 1224 Bedford Castle was the base of Falkes de Breauté, the illegitimate son of a Norman knight who had risen through his service to John and Henry III during the civil wars of 1215–17 to become one of the most powerful men in the kingdom. He controlled large tracts of land and numerous castles, some royal and others seized from rebels. Falkes (described as Falcasius in the following document) was almost inevitably resented on account of his humble, and foreign, origins. Like a considerable number of the men who held castles for John during the war he seems to have shown a marked reluctance to return them to their original owners once there was peace; he handed back most of the castles under his control in 1223 but held on to Bedford. The following year his brother William seized a royal judge, who had given a number of verdicts against the de Breautés, and imprisoned him in the castle. Roger of Wendover records how the royal army arrived at Bedford on 20 June, determined to give this foreign upstart his comeuppance:

The king, on his arrival there sent messengers to the chief castellans, asking admission and demanding the restoration of Henry de Braibroc, his justiciary. Willam de Breauté, however, brother of Falcasius, and the others of the garrison, told the messengers in reply that they would not give up the castle unless they had orders to do so from their lord Falcasius, especially as they were not bound by homage or allegiance to the king. When this answer was brought back to the king, he was very indignant, and in his anger, ordered his troops to surround the castle... Then the archbishop and all the bishops, with tapers lighted, laid the ban of excommunication on Falcasius, and all the garrison of the castle... By orders of the king the engines of war, such as petrariae and mangonels, were brought up and, being disposed around the city, the besieging army made constant fierce assaults on the castle; the besieged, however, bravely defended the walls, and sent forth showers of deadly missiles on the besiegers. To be brief, many were wounded and slain on both sides... the king being roused to anger, sore, by the soul of his father, that if the garrisons were made prisoners by force he would hang them all; they, however, being provoked to do further wrong by the king's threats, forbade the messengers of the king to speak to them again on the subject of giving up the castle. This deadly hatred increased from the numbers of the slain, so that brothers spared not brothers, nor fathers their children. At length, after great slaughter on both sides, the king's workmen constructed a high tower of wood, built on geometrical principles, in which they placed crossbowmen who could watch every proceeding in the castle; and from that time no one in the castle could take off his armour without being mortally wounded. The besieged, however, did not cease to strike down their enemies; for, to the confusion of the king's army, they killed two knights of his who exposed themselves to death too rashly, thus provoking the anger of their enemies against them by all means possible...

At length the king's soldiers brought up, though not without much loss, two penthouses which the French call brutesches and, attacking the castle in all directions, forced the besieged to retire. The king's troops then entered the castle, and gaining possession of horses, arms, provisions, and innumerable other things, returned in triumph; the victors then attacked the tower and destroyed a great portion of the walls. After this the besieged, seeing that they could hold out no longer, on the eve of the assumption of St Mary [14 August] sent some of the garrison from the castle to entreat the king's mercy; but the king ordered them to be kept in close confinement till he reduced the rest to subjection. On the following day all the rest came out of the castle dreadfully bruised and wounded, and were taken before the king who ordered them all to be hung; of the knights and soldiers of the garrison, twenty-four were hung, who could not obtain mercy from the king on account of the audacity which they had showed to him in the late siege...

Although Roger of Wendover mentions some of the equipment employed by the besiegers of Bedford Castle – catapults to bombard the walls, a siege tower to house crossbowmen, two penthouses for shelter – his account is not complete; for example, we know from other sources that both the inner bailey wall and the great tower itself were breached by miners, some of whom came from as far away as the Forest of Dean. In fact the use of miners is indicated by Roger when he mentions the two penthouses under which they would have sheltered. However, what this account does demonstrate with stark clarity is the rising animosity between the two sides as demands to surrender were rejected and casualties mounted. The siege began with a formal summons to surrender, which was rejected by the defenders. In an attempt to lower the garrison's morale the king then had them excommunicated by the Archbishop of Canterbury, a tactic to be repeated 40 years later at Kenilworth. When the defenders continued to resist they were told by the king that 'if the garrisons were made prisoners [by force] he would hang them all': in other words, if the defenders forced the king's army to storm the castle their lives would be forfeit. Knowing this but unwilling to surrender, the garrison fought desperately, inflicting heavy casualties on the king's men. Finally, with the castle collapsing about their ears, the defenders asked for mercy but, for 24 of them at least, it was too late. Falkes, who was not present at the siege, was exiled, his brother hanged and the castle demolished.

III **Scottish attack on Carlisle, 1315, from the** *Lanercost Chronicle*
In 1315, fresh from his victory at Bannockburn, Robert Bruce invaded England with a large Scottish army. The *Lanercost Chronicle* records the events:

A little later in the same year, on the feast of St Mary Magdalene [22 July], the King of Scotland, having mustered all his forces, came to Carlisle, invested the city and besieged it for ten days, trampling down all the crops, wasting the suburbs and all within the bounds, burning the whole of that district, and driving in a very great store of cattle for his army from Allerdale, Copland and Westmorland. On every day of the siege they assaulted one of the three gates of the city, sometimes three at once; but never without loss, because there were discharged upon them from the walls such dense volleys of darts and arrows, likewise stones, that they asked one another whether stones bred and multiplied within the walls. Now on the fifth day of the siege they set up a machine for casting stones next to the church of Holy Trinity, where their king stationed himself, and they cast great stones continually against the Caldew gate and against the wall, but they did little or no injury to those within except that they killed one man. But there were seven or eight similar machines within the city, besides other engines of war, which are called springalds, for discharging long darts, and staves with sockets for casting stones, which caused great fear and damage to those outside. Meanwhile, however, the Scots set up a certain great berefrai like a kind of tower, which was considerably higher than the city walls. On perceiving this, the carpenters of the city erected upon a tower of the wall, against which that engine must come if it ever reached the wall, a wooden tower loftier than the other; but neither that engine nor any other ever did reach the wall because, when it was being drawn on wheels over the wet and swampy ground, having stuck there through its own weight it could neither be taken any further nor do any harm.

Moreover the Scots had made many long ladders, which they brought with them for scaling the wall in different places simultaneously; also a sow for mining the town wall, had they been able; but neither sow nor ladders availed them aught. Also they made great numbers of fascines of corn and herbage to fill the moat outside the wall on the east side, so as they might pass over dry-shod. Also they made long bridges of logs running upon wheels, such as being strongly and swiftly drawn with ropes might reach across the width of the moat. But during all the time the Scots were on the ground neither fascines sufficed to fill the moat, nor those wooden bridges to cross the ditch, but sank to the depths by their own weight.

Howbeit on the ninth day of the siege, when all the machines were ready, they delivered a general assault upon all the city gates and upon the whole circuit of the wall, attacking manfully, while the citizens defended themselves just as manfully, and they did the same next day. The Scots also resorted to the same kind of stratagem whereby they had taken Edinburgh Castle; for they employed the greater part of their army in delivering an assault upon the eastern side of the city, against the place of the Minorite Friars, in order to draw thither the people who were inside. But Sir James of Douglas, a bold and cautious knight, stationed himself, with some others of the army who were most daring and nimble, on the west side opposite the place of the Canons and Preaching Friars, where no attack was expected because of the height [of the wall] *and the difficulty of access. There they set up long ladders which they climbed and the bowmen, whereof they had a great number, shot their arrows thickly to prevent anyone showing his head above the wall. But, blessed be God! they met with such resistance there as threw them to the ground with their ladders, so that there and elsewhere round the wall some were killed, others taken prisoners and others wounded; yet throughout the whole siege no Englishman was killed, save one man only who was struck by an arrow (and except the man above mentioned), and few were wounded.*

Whereof on the eleventh day, to wit the feast of St Peter ad Vincula [1 August], *whether because they had heard that the English were approaching to relieve the besieged or whether they despaired of success, the Scots marched off in confusion to their own country, leaving behind all their engines of war aforesaid...*

Despite their victory at Bannockburn in the previous year, the Scots generally avoided fighting pitched battles with the larger and better-equipped English forces and therefore needed to capture Carlisle quickly before a relief force arrived. As a result, there was no thought of attempting to starve the defenders into submission. Instead, many of the assault techniques discussed earlier were immediately employed: bombardment by siege engines; the construction of a siege tower; an attempt to undermine the city walls under the protection of a sow; simultaneous attacks in different places to stretch the defenders' resources; the employment of fascines and improvised bridges to cross the moat; diversionary attacks; and the use of scaling ladders while archers attempt-ed to keep the defenders' heads down. Given that less than two years earlier their main assault technique had been to climb up a ladder in the middle of the night, the fact that the Scots even attempted such a siege is evidence of how much their confidence had improved since Bannockburn. In the event, however, the Scots were unsuccessful. This was partly due to the actions of the English in the castle and city. Under the leadership of Sir Andrew Harclay they mounted a vigorous and active defence, bombarding the besiegers with stones from siege engines of their own and making ad hoc alterations to the defences of the city to counter Scottish moves. However, the true conqueror of the Scots that July may well have been the weather: it is said that it never stopped raining that summer. The ground became impossibly swampy and Bruce's hopes of taking Carlisle ended up, like his siege tower, hopelessly bogged down in the mud outside the city.

The *Lanercost Chronicle*'s account of the siege of Carlisle is vividly supplemented by a contemporary embellishment of Edward II's charter, grant-ed in 1316 in acknowledgement of its citizens' role in defending Carlisle against the Scots the previous year. Sir Andrew Harclay's role in leading the defence is attested by his prominent position in the illustration; identifiable by his coat of arms, he is the helmeted figure preparing to throw a spear from the battle-ments. Next to him a defender turns a windlass in order to draw back the spring of one of the dart-throwing springalds mentioned in the account. Other defenders hurl stones down onto a party of Scots who are using pickaxes in an attempt to undermine the city walls. One attacker has climbed a scaling lad-der only to be run through by a spear. To the left is a trebuchet, probably the 'machine for casting stones' used by the Scots to bombard the city's Caldew gate. Whereas the English wear coats of mail, the Scots are depicted without armour and one of the operators of the trebuchet has been pierced by a spear.

IV Supplying the siege at Kenilworth: the Liberate Rolls of 1266

Literally meaning 'deliver ye', the Liberate Rolls record writs authorising payments by the exchequer to sheriffs and other royal officials for specific purchases. These extracts paint a vivid picture of the scale, complexity and financial impact of the siege from the end of June.

June 28
To the Sheriff of Gloucester. Contrabreve to let Payn de Lydney have 20s without delay for 3 keels which he caused to be made and 10s for carriage of timber for the King's engines from the forest of Dean to the water of Lydney...

July 2
To the Sheriff of Gloucester. Contrabreve to find for John Malemort, Master of the King's Quarrels at St Briavels, the expenses necessary for the making of 6,000 quarrels for two feet crossbows, to receive them together with other quarrels which he will deliver, and carry them to the King at Kenilworth, the King having commanded him to make them and put them together day and night in all possible haste and deliver them by parcels to the sheriff to carry whither the King has enjoined; in no way failing hereof as he wishes to keep himself safe and avoid the King's indignation.

July 28
To the Sheriff of Gloucester. Contrabreve to carry the King's moveable tower which is at Gloucester, with all its gear, to the King at Kenilworth without delay and without fail.

July 28
To the Sheriff of Oxford. Contrabreve to make 500 hurdles, 8ft long 7ft wide, for the King in the forest of Bernewood and 1,000 in that of Wychwood and carry them to the King without delay and without fail.

To the Sheriff of Worcester. To make 500 similar hurdles in the forest of Feckenham and carry them to the King as above.

To the Sheriff of Northampton. To make 500 thick and close wattled hurdles 10ft by 8ft and carry them to Kenilworth as above.

August 2
To the Sheriff of Wiltshire. To receive 10 bucks which John Lovel and Henry of Candover, the King's huntsmen, will take in the forest of Cette, and 10 which they will take in that of Savernake, and salt them well and carry 10 bucks to Windsor for Eleanor, consort of Edward the King's firstborn, and the other 10 to the King at Kenilworth in all possible haste.

August 9
To William, son of Richard, Sheriff of London. Contrabreve to have made in the city of London 20,000 quarrels for crossbows for one foot and 10,000 for crossbows for two feet and send them in all possible haste to the King at Kenilworth, as he is in extreme need thereof for the present siege of the castle there.

September 4
To William, son of Richard, Sheriff of London. Let Maud, late wife of John le Picard, the King's crossbowman who lately died in the King's service at Kenilworth, and his 3 children, have 4d daily out of the issues of the city for their maintenance.

V John Barbour describes how in 1313 Sir James Douglas took Roxburgh Castle from the English

John Barbour was Archdeacon of Aberdeen and Auditor of the Exchequer to Robert II of Scotland. It was probably in the 1370s that he penned *The Bruce*, 13,000 lines of isosyllabic rhyming couplets telling the story of the Scottish struggle for independence from England earlier that century. Although he wrote with a patriotic purpose and clearly idealised the life and actions of Robert Bruce, the events in the poem seem generally to have been faithful to historical fact. This extract from a prose translation of the original early Scots text, made a century ago, deals with the capture of Roxburgh Castle by Bruce's lieutenant, Sir James Douglas. Lacking siege equipment, the Scots were forced to rely on subterfuge and surprise in their bid to capture castles from the English:

While, as I have said, the good Earl Thomas [Randolph] *besieged Edinburgh, James of Douglas set all his wit to discover how, by any craft or stratagem, Roxburgh could be taken. At length he caused Sim of the Leadhouse, a crafty and skilful man, to make ladders of hempen ropes with wooden steps, so bound that they should in no way break. They devised and made a hook of iron, strong and square which, if it once fixed on a battlement with the ladder straitly stretched from it, should hold securely.*

As soon as this was devised and done the Lord of Douglas, in secret, gathered trusty men – I trow there might be three score of them – and on Fastern's Even [Shrove Tuesday, 27 February 1313], *in the beginning of the night, took the road for the castle. They covered all the armour they wore with black frocks. Soon they came near the castle; they then sent all their horses back and went along the path in single file on hands and feet, as if they were cows and oxen that had been left out unsecured.*

It was very dark, without a doubt; nevertheless one of the garrison, who lay on the wall, said to his fellow beside him, 'this man', and he named a small farmer near the place, 'thinks to make good cheer, for he has left all his oxen out.' The other said, 'no doubt it is so. He makes merry tonight, though they should be driven off by the Douglas.'

They supposed the Douglas and his men were oxen because they went on hands and feet, always one by one. Douglas took right good heed to all they said, but soon they passed indoors, talking as they went.

Douglas's men were glad of this and sped swiftly to the wall, and soon set up their ladders. But one made a sound when the hook fastened hard in the battlement. This was clearly heard by one of the watchmen and he instantly made for the spot. Leadhouse, who had made the ladder, hastened to be first to climb the wall, but, ere he had quite got up, the warder met him and, thinking to throw him down without noise, cry or sound, dashed quickly at him. Then Leadhouse, who was in hazard of his life, made a leap at him and got him by the throat and stabbed him upwards with a knife till he took the life in his hand. And when he saw him lie dead he went forthwith upon the wall and cast the body down to his fellows, and said, 'all goes as we wish; speed quickly up!'

This they hastened to do, but before they came up a man came along and saw Leadhouse standing alone, and knew he was not of the garrison. This man rushed at him and attacked him stoutly but was quickly slain, for Leadhouse was armed and active and the other had no armour and nothing to stop a stroke.

Thus Leadhouse did battle upon the wall till Douglas and his company were come up. Then they went quickly into the tower. At that moment the garrison were all in the hall, dancing, singing and otherwise at play, as is the joyous and glad custom upon Fastern's Even among folk in safety, as they believed themselves to be. But, ere they knew, Douglas and all his men poured into the hall, crying aloud, 'Douglas! Douglas!' And they were more in number than he, [yet] when they heard the dreadful shout of 'Douglas!' they were dismayed and set up no right defence. Douglas's men slew them without mercy till they got the upper hand and the garrison, fearing death beyond measure, fled seeking safety. The warden, Gylmyne de Fiennes, saw how it went and got into the great tower with others of his company and hastily closed the gate. The rest, who were left outside, were taken or slain, except some who leapt the wall.

That night Douglas held the hall, to the sorrow of his enemies. His men kept going to and fro throughout the castle all that night till daylight on the morrow. The warden in the tower, Gylmyne de Fiennes, was a man of great valour, and when he saw the castle altogether lost he set his force to defend the keep. Those without sent arrows in upon him in such number that he was greatly distressed; nevertheless, he held the tower stubbornly till the next day. Then, in an attack, he was wounded so badly in the face that he feared for his life. For this reason he speedily made parley, and yielded *the tower on condition that he and all with him should pass safely to England. Douglas kept good faith with them and conveyed them to their own country, but de Fiennes lived there but a short time for, by reason of the wound in his face, he soon died and was buried.*

VI The Hundred Years War: the siege of Breteuil described by Froissart

Jean Froissart was born in the Low Countries in about 1337. In 1360 he became a protégé of Philippa of Hainault, Queen of England, and spent about six years in the country. He visited the court of David II of Scotland and in 1366 he accompanied Edward the Black Prince on campaign in France. Froissart also travelled widely in France, the Low Countries and Italy. Written in French prose, his chronicle deals with the history of western Europe from 1327 to 1400, the first half based on the accounts of an earlier chronicler, Jean le Bel. Froissart's accuracy is frequently open to question but his chronicles remain a superb evocation of the age.

This extract deals with John II of France's siege, in 1356, of Breteuil in eastern Normandy, which was defended by followers of Edward III's ally, Charles of Navarre.

If Froissart's account is accurate it marks something of a watershed in siege warfare, for as well as being an early example of the use of cannon, it was also one of the last times that a mobile siege tower was employed:

You should know that the French who were before Breteuil hastened to devise a variety of means of attack to exhaust the garrison. The knights and squires inside strove night and day to counter them. The besiegers constructed great engines which hurled missiles by day and night against the roofs of the towers and caused much damage. The King of France also ordered carpenters to build a large, three-storey belfry or wooden tower, which could be moved on wheels. Each storey could hold at least 200 men, with room for them to brandish their weapons. This tower had loopholes and was padded with leather to protect it... While it was being constructed the local peasants were ordered to bring up large quantities of wood, unload them in the moat and then cover them with straw and earth so that the tower could be wheeled against the walls... It took a full month for the moat to be filled at the spot where the attack was to take place. When everything was ready, a large force of knights and squires, anxious for glory, entered the tower which was then pushed on its four wheels towards the walls.

The garrison had seen the tower being constructed and had established in their minds what the French planned to do. As a result they had equipped themselves with cannons that could shoot both fire and large, heavy bolts that could cause great destruction. They prepared themselves to attack the tower and defend themselves bravely. First, before firing their cannons, they battled with the men in the tower in hand-to-hand combat. Many fine feats-of-arms took place. When they felt they had done enough of this they began firing their cannons, launching fire on top of and inside the tower, together with volleys of their great bolts. Many of the besiegers were killed and wounded and the others so beset that they did not know which way to turn. The fire, which was Greek Fire, set light to the roof of the tower, forcing those inside to abandon it hurriedly for fear of perishing in the flames. When the defenders of Breteuil saw this, they raised a great cheer...

What was left of the tower remained in the moat and no attempt was made to use it again. But the French carried on filling the rest of the moat, using fifteen hundred men who every day did nothing else...

The defenders of Breteuil negotiated a surrender with the King of France, for the siege-engines which were in continuous action were causing great damage and there was no sign of relief from any quarter. They knew that if Breteuil was taken by storm they would all be massacred without mercy. On his part, the King of France was anxious to lead his troops against the English who were laying waste to his country and was also tired of sitting before that fortress with sixty thousand men whom he was maintaining at great expense. He therefore agreed to spare their lives and let them depart with whatever possessions they could carry, but nothing else. The knights and squires of Breteuil made for Cherbourg with a safe-conduct from the king. The king took possession of the castle which he had thoroughly repaired. He then struck camp and headed for Paris, but kept all his men-at-arms with him as he expected to have further use for them.

VII The use of spies, by John Cruso

For both besieger and besieged, spies were an invaluable weapon in siege warfare. Inside information about a castle's strengths and weaknesses could be crucial in planning an attack, while the knowledge of where and when an assault was planned could make all the difference in repelling it. Furthermore, an awareness of the opposition's situation and intentions could immeasurably strengthen a commander's hand in the bluff and counter-bluff of surrender negotiations. Both sides used spies during the siege of Wardour; Corfe fell to the Parliamentarians through treachery; and, if a Parliamentarian account of its capture is to be believed, the Royalists may well have been shown the best way into Beeston by someone inside the castle. One of the most popular of the many books on the art of war produced in 17th-century England was John Cruso's *Militarie Instructions for the Cavall'rie*, which was originally published in 1632 and reprinted in 1644. In it Cruso draws attention to the importance of intelligence and the value of spies:

Of spies
The best and principal means for a commander to avoid divers
inconveniences and to effect many worthy designs are, first, to be sure to
keep his own deliberations and resolutions secret. Secondly, to penetrate
the designs and intentions of the enemy. For which purpose it behoves him
to have good spies, which must be exceedingly well rewarded so that they
may be the readier to expose themselves to all dangers. The best and most
assured spies are one's own soldiers which (feigning some discontent for
want of pay or otherwise) enter into the enemy's service and get themselves
into the cavalry, as having best opportunity (whether in the field or in
garrison) to give information. Of these it is good to have many and in
several places, the one knowing nothing of the other. You are to agree with
them of the place where they shall convey their letters, as some tree, gallows
or other place easy to find, where they also shall find yours, giving them
order to come in person when their advice is of great importance: as, if the
enemy would fall upon a quarter, surprise some place or attempt some
other great enterprise. There might also divers soldiers be daily sent
disguised, under several pretences, to observe what is done in the enemy's
leaguer, when it is near. The boors [peasants] use also to serve for spies, as
well women as men, which, being not much regarded nor suspected, may

have the freer access; but these are not always to be trusted, neither are they so well able to judge of or to pierce into business, and the less assurance and information is to be had by their relation.

There are also spies which are called double, which must be men of great fidelity. These (to get credit with the enemy) must sometimes give him true information of what passes on the other side; but of such things, and at such times, as they may do no hurt. But this kind of spies cannot continue long without being discovered.

If it be possible, such spies must be had as are entertained into domestic service of the chief officers of the enemy, the better to know their intentions and designs.

On the other side, there must be exceeding great care taken to beware of the enemy's spies, which otherwise may do you as much mischief as you reap benefit by your own.

VIII The siege of Gloucester, 1643, by John Corbet

The failure by the Royalists to capture the city of Gloucester in the late summer of 1643 has been seen by many as the turning point of the First Civil War. The Royalists needed to control the city in order to open safe communications between their capital at Oxford and the fertile recruiting grounds of south Wales. After capturing Bristol on 26 July 1643 the Royalists laid siege to Gloucester and Charles I himself appeared before the city on 10 August. However its governor, Colonel Edward Massey, refused to capitulate and held out until 8 September, when the city was relieved by an army from London under the Earl of Essex. This account of the siege was penned two years after the event by John Corbet, a Puritan divine who was Colonel Massie's chaplain. Although dealing with the siege of a city, not a castle, and clearly biased in favour of the defenders, Corbet's narrative illustrates many of the aspects of a 'formal' siege. The Royalists use mortar fire to cause destruction and lower morale, and attempt to breach the city walls through bombardment and mining. For their part the defenders make improvised repairs to their defences, snipe at the besiegers and launch raids on the enemy's siege works.

The enemy ... chose not a sudden storm on the lower and weaker parts of the city, but rather to prepare the assault on the strongest side, yet most easy to their intention. For there only could they raise the works without the annoyance of the water springs that issued in the lower grounds; there only could they make batteries within pistol shot of the walls that wanted flankers; and when they had once entered a breach there, they were instantly possessed of the highest part of the town. On this side therefore were their ordnance brought up, and first two culverins of sixteen pound bullet were planted on the east side, a little out of musket shot where they made some store of shot, but did no execution. Next they planted three pieces of ordnance of fourteen and five-and-twenty pound bullet upon their battery in a square redoubt, on the south side, and began to batter the corner point of the wall and a brick house adjoining, where one of our men was killed, without more harm. Then they played upon our ordnance mounted against their battery point blank, and made some slight breach which was quickly stopped up with woolpacks and cannon baskets. By this time they had drawn the trench near the moat, where they made a kind of mine to drain it, and sunk much of the water: and attempted to cast faggots into the moat but were beaten off by our musketeers. At several times they shot large granadoes out of their mortar pieces. Many fell into houses and broke, but did no harm, and one that fell in the street had the fuze quenched before it came to ground, was taken up whole and found to weigh three score pound...

The enemy having planted three pieces of ordnance against the south side, and now three more on the east side and two more near the east gate within pistol shot of the town wall, began a most furious battery upon the corner point and made above a hundred and fifty great shot against it, whereby the stones were sorely battered but the earthworks stood firm. By all this shot only two persons were hurt, for the battery was so near that if the bullet missed the wall it flew quite over the town, or lighted at random, yet in the intervals of the great shot after each discharge our musketeers played hard and killed four principal cannoneers. Neither were the people daunted at the noise of the cannon, which by the slender execution became so contemptible that at every time women and children wrought hard in lining the walls and repairing the breaches...

The enemy still prepared for a general storm, meanwhile seeking to waste our magazine which they knew must needs suddenly fail, expended their own store, and daily acted to the terror of the inhabitants; shooting granadoes, fireballs and great stones out of their mortar pieces, and had now planted a battery on the south side westward, unto which the lower part of the town was open. Thence in one night they shot above twenty fiery melting hot iron bullets, some eighteen pound weight, others two-and-twenty pound weight, which were seen to fly through the air like the shooting of a star. They passed through stables and ricks of hay, where the fire by the swiftness of the motion did not catch, and falling on the tops of houses presently melted the leads and sunk through; but all the skill and industry of the enemy could not set one house on fire.

They still played their great shot against the walls, and wrought hard in filling up the moat with faggots and earth at the place where they battered, where they also built a gallery over the head of the trench, the breadth of four abreast; in the shelter thereof they had almost worked themselves over the moat. Then we found that they had sunk a mine under the East Gate; whereupon the Governor commanded a countermine in two places, but finding the springs left off, conceiving for the same reason the endeavour of the enemy to no purpose. To discover or interrupt this work, a sergeant with five daring men were put forth at a port hole in the dungeon at the East Gate, came close to the mouth of the mine, took off the board that covered it, and for a while viewed the miners. One of these cast in a hand granado amongst them, whilst the four musketeers played upon them as they ran forth, and with the noise of the men from the walls gave the whole leaguer a strong alarm and crept in at the port hole without harm. Wherefore, discovering that the enemy, notwithstanding the springs, went on with their mine, we renewed our countermine; for they had sunk a great depth under the moat and extremely toiled in drawing up the spring water, till at length they had gotten under the gate that our miners could hear them work under them, and did expect to spoil them by pouring in water, or stealing out their powder.

For a remedy to this mischief and withal the enemy having planted store of cannon baskets within half musket shot of the East Gate point blank, intending a battery there upon the springing of the mine; we made a very strong work across the street with a large trench before it and filled it with water, intending to raise it up to the eaves of the houses and to plant some cannon there: we answered their several approaches by so many counterworks. A sconce was built upon a rising ground that looked into their trenches, where we could plant four piece of ordnance to clear within the walls a ground called the Friar's Orchard southward, and secure their flank upon their entrance at the East Gate, and so northward. Also an inner work was drawn from the south side along the middle of the orchard and all passages stopped between that and the East port. And to hinder their gallery we began to undermine for a place to put forth a piece of ordnance at the bottom of the wall, to batter the flank thereof; which was perfected and a saker there placed. Commanded men were drawn out upon the walls, granadoes provided and, when the great gun played upon the gallery, the musketeers sent plenty of shot and cast divers granadoes into their trenches; in the meanwhile (they firing their ordnance against the top of the wall) we cut off a main beam of the gallery with our bolt shot. But the same day the enemy had sunk a piece against the port hole of our mine and forced us to withdraw the saker, yet we cast them back three days work.

IX The storming of Shelford House, November 1645, described by Lucy Hutchinson

In November 1645 Colonel Sydenham Poyntz, the Parliamentarian major-general of the northern counties, was ordered to blockade the Royalist stronghold of Newark until the Scots could come south to besiege it. However, before this could be done two outlying Royalist garrisons, at Shelford and Wiverton, had first to be reduced. Poyntz was joined before Shelford by forces under the command of Colonel John Hutchinson, the Parliamentarian governor of Nottingham and future regicide. In 1638 Hutchinson had married Lucy Apsley, the daughter of Sir Allen Apsley one-time governor of the Tower of London, and sister of Sir Allen Apsley Junior, a leading Royalist. A fervent Puritan, Lucy Hutchinson remained at her husband's side throughout the Civil War. After her husband's death (ironically as a prisoner in the Tower of London in 1664) she wrote a lively and well-informed narrative of his life, from which this superb account of the storming of Shelford House is drawn.

In a bid to secure Shelford without bloodshed, Hutchinson (referred to by his wife as 'the governor' throughout the account) wrote to Philip Stanhope, its Royalist governor, offering him generous terms of surrender. After he received what Lucy Hutchinson describes as 'a very scornful huffing reply' the Parliamentarians prepared to storm the house. Serving alongside John Hutchinson was his brother George (described as 'the lieutenant-colonel' in Hutchinson's account) and Charles White, a captain of dragoons who, as the account makes clear, was something of a rival. Lucy Hutchinson vividly describes the Parliamentarians' struggle to force their way into the house and the chaos that reigned once they did. Religious animosities made the fighting particularly bitter and, having refused to surrender, the garrison were not entitled to quarter by the laws of war of the time. Many were put to the sword on Poyntz's orders. In the confusion Hutchinson himself was nearly attacked by some Parliamentarians who, not knowing who he was and hearing him called 'the governor' by his men, assumed he was the Royalist commander.

The governor being armed and ready to begin the assault, when the rest were also ready, Captain White came to him and, notwithstanding all his former malicious prosecutions, now pretended the most tender care and love that could be declared, with all imaginable flattery; and persuaded the governor not to hazard himself in so dangerous an attempt but to consider his wife and children and stand by among the horse, but by no means to storm the place in his own person. Notwithstanding all his false insinuations the governor, perceiving his envy at that honour which his valour was ready to reap in this encounter, was exceedingly angry with him and went on upon the place. This being seated on a flat, was encompassed with a very strong bulwark and a great ditch without, in most places wet at the bottom so that they within were very confident of being able to hold it out, there being no cannon brought against them; because also a broken regiment of the queen's, who were all papists, were come in to their assistance. A regiment of Londoners was appointed to storm on the other side, and the governor at the same time began the assault at his post.

His men found many more difficulties than they expected, for after they had filled up the ditches with faggots and pitched the scaling ladders, they were twenty staves too short and the enemy, from the top of the works, threw down logs of wood which would sweep off a whole ladderful of men at once: the lieutenant-colonel himself was once or twice so beaten down. The governor had ordered other musketeers to beat off those men that stood upon the top of the works, which they failed to do by shooting without good aim. But the governor directed them better and the Nottingham horse, dismounting and assailing them with their pistols and headpieces, helped the foot to beat them all down from the top of the works, except one stout man who stood alone and did wonders in beating down the assailants. The governor being angry at this fetched two of his own musketeers and made them shoot and he immediately fell, to the great discouragement of his fellows.

Then the governor himself first entered, and the rest of his men came in as fast as they could. But while this regiment was entering on this side, the Londoners were beaten off on the other side and the main force of the garrison turned upon him. The cavaliers had half moons [defensive earthworks] within, which were as good a defence to them as their first works. Into these the soldiers that were of the queen's regiment were gotten, and they in the house shot from out of all the windows. The governor's men, as soon as they got in, took the stables and all their horses, but the governor himself was fighting with the captain of the papists and some others who, by advantage of the half moon and the house, might have prevailed to cut him off and those that were with him, which were not many. The enemy, being strengthened by the addition of those who had beaten off the assailants on the other side, were now trying their utmost to vanquish those that were within. The lieutenant-colonel, seeing his brother in hazard, made haste to open the drawbridge, that Poyntz might come in with his horse; which he did, but not before the governor had killed that gentleman who was fighting with him, at whose fall his men gave way.

Poyntz, seeing them shoot from the house and apprehending the king might come to their relief, when he came in, ordered that no quarter should be given. And here the governor was in greater danger than before, for the strangers hearing him called governor were advancing to have killed him, but that the lieutenant-colonel, who was very watchful to preserve him all that day, came in to his rescue. He scarcely could persuade them that it was the Governor of Nottingham; because he, at the beginning of the storm, had put off a very good suit of armour that he had, which being musket-proof was so heavy that it heated him, and so would not be persuaded by his friends to wear anything but his buff coat. The governor's men, eager to complete their victory, were forcing their entrance into the house. Meanwhile Rossiter's men came and took away all their horses, which they had taken away when they first entered the works and won the stables, and left in the guard of two or three, while they were pursuing their work.

The Governor of Shelford, after all his bravadoes, came but meanly off; it is said that he sat in his chamber, wrapped up in his cloak, and came not forth that day; but that availed him not, for how or by whom it is not known, but he was wounded and stripped and flung upon a dunghill. The lieutenant-colonel, after the house was mastered, seeing the disorder by which our men were ready to murder one another, upon the command Poyntz had issued to give no quarter, desired Poyntz to cause the slaughter to cease, which was presently obeyed, and about seven score prisoners were saved. While he was thus busied, enquiring what was begun of the governor, he was shown him naked upon the dunghill; whereupon the lieutenant-colonel called for his own cloak and cast it over him and sent him to a bed in his own quarters, and procured him a surgeon... Though he had all the supplies they could every way give him, he died the next day.

The house, which belonged to his father, the Earl of Chesterfield, was that night burned, none certainly knowing by what means, whether by accident or on purpose; but there was most ground to believe that the country people, who had been sorely infested by that garrison, to prevent the keeping of it by those who had taken it, purposely set it on fire. If the queen's regiment had mounted their horses and stood ready upon them when our men entered, they had undoubtedly cut them all off; but they standing to the works, it pleased God to lead them into that path he had ordained for their destruction who, being papists, would not receive quarter, nor were they much offered it, being killed in the heat of the contest so that not a man of them escaped.

The next day our party went to Wiverton, a house of the Lord Chaworth's which, terrified with the example of the other, yielded upon terms and was by order pulled down and rendered incapable of being any more a garrison.

X Pendennis terms of surrender

*Articles agreed on the 16th of August, Anno Dom 1646, between Sir
Abraham Shipman, Lieut-Col Richard Arundel, Col William Slaughter,
Col Charles Jennings, Col Lewis Tremain, Nevil Bligh and Joseph June,
Esq, Lieut-Col Anthony Brocket, on the behalf of the Honourable John
Arundel of Trerise, Esq, Governor of the Castle of Pendennis, of the one
party: and Col John St Aubin, Esq, High Sheriff of the County of
Cornwall, Sir John Ayscue, Knt, Col Robert Bennet, Lieut-Col Edward
Herle, Lieut-Col Thomas Fitch, Lieut-Col Richard Townsend, Major
Thomas Jennings and Capt Walter Maynard, on the behalf of the
Honourable Col Richard Fortescue, Commander-in-Chief under his
Excellency Sir Thomas Fairfax, of all the forces of horse and foot within
the County of Cornwall; and the Honourable Capt William Batten, Vice-
Admiral and Commander-in-Chief of the whole fleet employ'd for the
service of King and Parliament, on the other party.*
*1. That the Castle of Pendennis, with all fortresses, forts, fortifications,
thereunto belonging, the ships and all other vessels lying under the castle,
with the furniture and provisions unto them appertaining, all ordnance of
all sorts, with all their equipage, and all arms, ammunition, provisions
and all other implements of war, necessaries and commodities of and
belonging to the said castle and garrison (except what otherwise shall be
disposed by these articles), shall without any manner of diminution, spoil
or embezzlement, be deliver'd upon Monday the 17th day of this instant
August, at two of the clock in the afternoon, into the hands and custody of
the two commanders-in-chief by land and sea respectively, or such person
or persons as shall be by them appointed for the receiving of the same. And
that immediately upon signing the said Articles, the said persons shall be
admitted into the castle, to see the just performance of the premises, and
hostages given for the due observance of them.*
*2. That John Arundel of Trerise, Esq, governor of the said castle of
Pendennis, with his family and retinue, and all officers and soldiers of
horse and foot, and all the train of artillery, and of the ships, as well
reformado'd officers* [officers with no soldiers to command, but who
kept their rank] *as others; and all gentlemen, clergymen, and their
families and servants, shall march out of the castle of Pendennis, with their
horses, compleat arms and other equipages, according to their present or*

past commands and qualities, with flying colours, trumpets sounding, drums beating, matches lighted at both ends, bullets in their mouths, and every soldier twelve charges of powder, with bullets and match proportionable, with all their own proper goods, bag and baggage, with a safe convoy unto Arnwich Downs. And because his Majesty hath neither army nor garrison in England to our knowledge, they shall there lay down their arms (saving their swords) unless such who are officers in commission, who with their servants are to retain their arms according to their qualities; country gentlemen and their servants their swords, only ensigns their colours; where such persons as Col Fortescue shall appoint, are to receive them; and as many as desire it are to have passes from the commanders-in-chief to pass to their several dwellings, or to such other places under the power of the Parliament, or beyond the seas, as they shall desire, and not be plunder'd, searched, or injur'd in their march, or after, they not doing anything to the prejudice of the Parliament's affairs; and no man to be prejudic'd for the giving any of the persons comprised in the said Articles, entertainment in their houses: and that the old garrison-soldiers who have houses in the castle shall have 28 days after the surrender, for the removing and disposing of their goods.

3. That the prince's servants with their arms, and all commanders, officers, gentlemen, ladies, gentlewomen, clergymen, and all others, with their retinue, that desire it, shall have liberty to pass with their bag and baggage and what else is allow'd in the Articles, beyond the seas; and to that purpose there shall be provided by the Vice-Admiral a sufficient number of navigable vessels, with a convoy for their safe transporting from the Haven of Falmouth, within 28 days after the surrender of the said castle, to be landed at St Maloes in France; and in the mean time to be assigned free quarters at convenient places by Col Fortescue, Commander-in-Chief; and during the said time that they be not plunder'd or injur'd, they acting nothing prejudicial to the Parliament's affairs.

4. That Col Wise and all officers and soldiers of his regiment, or as many of them as desire it, be shipt in Falmouth Harbour, in vessels to be provided by the Vice-Admiral, and landed at Swansey in Wales: and those such as are of the county of Cornwall be shipt and landed at Looe; and those that be of Devon be landed at Yalme; and all to be shipt with bag and baggage and such arms as formerly allowed them, nor to be plunder'd nor injur'd in their passage.

5. *That whereas by reason of the long siege of the castle of Pendennis, many of the officers and soldiers of the said garrison are grown into great necessity of all such things as might enable them to march to their several dwellings, many sick and wounded; and to the intent they may be supplied with necessaries for their accommodations within the time limited to them by these Articles, it is promised and consented unto the Commissioners for the Leaguer, to and with the Commissioners within the castle, that five hundred pounds Sterling shall be deliver'd into the hands of the Commissioners of the castle, or any three of them, at 8 of the clock tomorrow morning at Penrin, to be distributed among the officers and soldiers aforesaid as they shall think fit; and they are not to take any free quarter in their marches.*

6. *That any goods taken from any person for the accommodation of this garrison or any person therein, shall be restored to their proper owners, or such as they shall appoint; and all goods now in the castle that properly belong to any other persons shall be restored to the owners thereof: and if any person carry away any goods not properly belonging unto him, and deny to deliver them upon demand, in presence of any officer in commission, he shall lose his bag and baggage and have such punishment as the now Governor of the Castle and the Commander-in-Chief, or any two of them, shall think fit: but all persons may retain whatsoever was taken from persons in arms, as lawful prize of war.*

7. *That the Governor, and all field officers, with their several retinues, shall be allow'd carriage by sea and land, to carry away their said goods to any place within their country.*

8. *That no officer, soldier or other person comprised within these Articles, shall be reproached, or have any disgraceful words or affronts offered, or be stopt, searched, plunder'd or injur'd in their marches, rendezvous, quarters, journeys, places of abode, or passages by sea or land; and if any such thing be done, satisfaction to be made according to the judgement of any two Commissioners or more, being of equal number of each party: nor shall any of the persons aforesaid be compell'd to take up arms against the King, nor be imprison'd for any cause of public or private concernment, during the space of 28 days after the surrender of the said castle; nor for any cause of public concernment, for 28 days after the said 28 days are ended.*

9. *That if any person within the garrison be sick or wounded, that they*

cannot take the benefit of the Articles at present, they shall have liberty to stay and be provided for at convenient places until they recover, and then they shall have the fruit and benefit of these Articles.

10. That all persons comprised in this capitulation shall enjoy their estates, real and personal, they submitting to all orders and ordinances of Parliament, and shall fully enjoy the benefit of these Articles.

11. That all prisoners of war of either side be set at liberty: and that liberty be given immediately after the surrender of the said castle to the Governor thereof, to give notice to their friends of the surrender of the said castle; and that no vessel coming with relief within ten days after the surrender shall be made prize.

12. That if any of these Articles shall in any point be broke or violated by any person or persons in Pendennis or comprised within this capitulation, the fault and punishment shall be upon them or him only who made the breach or violation, and shall not be imputed or charged on any not assenting thereunto, or acting therein.

13. That all persons comprised in these Articles, shall upon request have certificates under the hands of the Commander-in-Chief respectively, that such persons were in the castle at the time of the surrender thereof, and were otherwise to have the benefit of these Articles.

14. That the Commanders-in-Chief respectively shall give passes to one or two messengers with their servants, not exceeding six, to go to the King by sea or land, from the Governor, to give an account to him of the proceedings of this treaty and conclusion thereof; and to return and receive the benefit of these Articles.

15. That Commissioners be appointed on both sides for the performance of the Articles, and places appointed for the accommodation of sick men.

16. That confirmation of all the precedent Articles shall be procured from the Parliament, or from his Excellency Sir Thomas Fairfax, within forty days after the signing of these Articles.

The terms of surrender given to the Royalists at Pendennis are a good example of what was known at the time as the 'honours of war'. Although they are obliged to hand over the castle with all the provisions and ordnance in it, the garrison are allowed to leave the castle as undefeated soldiers, with their horses, colours and personal weapons – the phrases 'matches lighted at both ends' and 'bullets in their mouths' refer to this. They are allowed to go free, either to their homes or to exile overseas, and are even offered transport in Parliamentarian ships. They are given money to assist with their various journeys and they are not to be insulted, searched or plundered. Members of the garrison who are too weak or sick to take advantage of the terms are to be looked after until they recover and no ship coming with supplies for the garrison can be captured for ten days.

Why did the Parliamentarians allow the garrison such generous terms? The Royalist Earl of Clarendon claimed that the garrison's stubborn resistance led the Parliamentarians to overestimate their strength. However, it seems far more likely that the Parliamentarians were generous because they could afford to be. They were anxious to bring hostilities to an end, and if that could be done without spending more time camped out in front of Pendennis, or losing men in a costly assault, then so much the better. In most circumstances a besieging commander would weigh up the pros and cons of allowing defenders to march away unmolested in exchange for a more rapid surrender. After all, the men could be used to reinforce the enemy's field army or strengthen another, perhaps more important, garrison. But Arundel's men had nowhere to go. There was no longer a Royalist army for them to join, no garrison in need of reinforcement. For the Royalists the right to march out of the castle with their arms and equipment onto the nearby Arnwich Down was purely symbolic, as Article 2 of the surrender terms points out:

> '...because his Majesty hath neither army nor garrison in England to our knowledge, they shall there lay down their arms (saving their swords).'

The Parliamentarians were aware that most of the starving and sickly garrison were by now looking for an excuse to surrender. By offering such generous terms they in effect made the exhausted Royalists an offer they could not refuse.

XI Goodrich terms of surrender

... they took in their standard colours, and held out their white flag of truce, and begged that they might march out honourably to their own homes, and some to garrisons. But nothing would be granted more than quarter for their lives. And in short it was agreed to thus:

First, that Sir Henry Lingen the Governor of Gotheridge Castle, with all the officers and soldiers therein, shall have mercy for their lives. Secondly, that the said Sir Henry Lingen the Governor, with all the officers and soldiers, shall surrender up themselves as prisoners to be at Colonel Birch his disposing. Thirdly, that all the arms and ammunition, provision, and whatsoever else is in Gotheridge Castle, shall be delivered up to Colonel Birch for the service of the Parliament. Fourthly, that the same be performed presently the same day (viz. July 31, 1646).

Your most humble servant N H, Gotheridge, July 31, 1646

In contrast to the detailed terms of surrender obtained by the Royalist defenders of Pendennis, these terms are brief and to the point and offer Lingen and his men nothing more than a promise to spare their lives. Lingen and his men are to become prisoners, Birch has the right to deal with them as he pleases and the defenders are to lose not only their weapons, ammunition and provisions, but also their property. The harshness of these terms can be attributed to two main factors. Firstly, Lingen's men had made a thorough nuisance of themselves during the previous year with the result that there seems to have been a certain amount of ill-feeling between the two forces, a fact alluded to when Birch initially summoned the garrison to surrender. Religion may well have played its part in heightening this animosity for Lingen and many of his fellow soldiers seem to have been Catholics. Secondly, the collapse of the north-west tower left the castle open to attack and fatally weakened the defenders' bargaining position. Knowing that if the Parliamentarians stormed the castle there was a very real chance that at least some of them would be put to the sword, the defenders had little alternative than to accept the terms, harsh as they were.

XII A comparison between the firelock and the musket, by Roger Earl of Orrery, 1677

Accounts of the Royalist capture of Beeston in 1643 and John Birch's raid on Goodrich specifically state that the assaults were made by soldiers armed with firelocks. A firelock (or flintlock) musket was fired by the sparks created when its flint struck steel. It was considerably less complicated to operate than the matchlock muskets with which the majority of musketeers were equipped and which were fired when a piece of burning cord, or match, ignited some powder in the musket's pan. In his *Treatise of the Art of War*, published in 1677, Roger Boyle 1st Earl of Orrery, a veteran of the wars in Ireland, explains the advantages of the firelock:

I would recommend the firelock musket above the matchlock musket, for several reasons; some of which I shall mention.

First, it is exceedingly more ready; for with the firelock you have only to cock and you are prepared to shoot but with your matchlock you have several motions, the least of which is as long a performing as but that one of the other, and oftentimes much more hazardous; besides, if you fire not the matchlock musket as soon as you have blown your match (which often, especially in hedge fights and sieges, you cannot do) you must a second time blow your match, or the ashes it gathers hinders it from firing.

Secondly, the match is very dangerous, either where bandoliers are used, or where soldiers run hastily in fight to the budge barrel, to refill their bandoliers; I have often seen sad instances thereof.

Thirdly, marching in the night to avoid an enemy, or to surprise one, or to assault a fortress, the matches often discover you and informs the enemy where you are; whereby you suffer much, and he obtains much.

Fourthly, in wet weather the pan of the musket being made wide open for a while, the rain often deads the powder and the match too; and in windy weather blows away the powder ere the match can touch the pan: nay, often in very high winds I have seen the sparks blown from the match, fire the musket ere the soldier meant it, and either thereby lose his shot, or wound or kill some one before him. Whereas in the firelock the motion is so sudden, that what makes the cock fall on the hammer strikes the fire and opens the pan at once.

Lastly, to omit many reasons, the quantity of match used in an army does much add to the baggage; and being of a very dry quality naturally draws the moisture of the air, which makes it relax and consequently less fit, though carried in close wagons: but if you march without wagons the match is the more exposed, and without being dried again in ovens is but half the use which otherwise it would be of: and which is full as bad, the skeins you give the corporals and the links you give the private soldiers (of which near an enemy, or on the ordinary guard duty, they must never be unfurnished) if they lodge in huts or tents, or if they keep guard in the open field (as most often it happens), all the match for instant service is too often rendered uncertain or useless; nothing of all which can be said of the flint, but much of it to the contrary.

And then the soldiers generally wearing their links of match near the bottom of the belt on which their bandoliers are fastened, in wet weather generally spoil the match they have; and if they are to fight on a sudden, and in the rain, you lose the use of your small shot which is sometimes of irreparable prejudice.

XIII Loading an artillery piece, by Benjamin Robins, 1742

Born in Bath in 1707, Benjamin Robins was a talented mathematician who wrote in support of the theories of Sir Isaac Newton. After teaching in London for some time he turned his hand to engineering and the study of fortification. He invented the ballistic pendulum, a device for measuring the velocity of a projectile, and in 1742 he published his best known work *New Principles of Gunnery* from which this extract is taken. Although it was written a hundred years after the outbreak of the English Civil War, the drill he describes here would have been more than familiar to a 17th-century siege-gun detachment. A 'budge barrel' was a small powder barrel with a leather liner that could be tied up for safety, while a 'linstock' was a stick used to fire cannon; it had a length of lighted match attached to one end and was pointed at the other so it could be stuck in the ground... downwind of any gunpowder!

Have in readiness powder, bullets, linstocks, scourers, rammers and the rest of your things. Stick up your linstock to leeward of you, then to work with your piece. First, clear your piece within with your scourer and see that the touch hole be clear and not stopped, and so clear that no dirt or filth be in the same. Then let him that is by to assist (for a piece cannot be managed by less than two) bring the budge barrel with the powder just before the mouth of your piece. Put then your ladle into the same and fill it, and if it be overfull give it a little jog, that the overplus may fall again into the barrel. After this, put it gently in at the mouth of the piece; even until the end of the ladle be thrust up to the breech-end of the piece. Then you must turn the ladle gently and softly and let it lie within the chamber of the piece. Drawing out your ladle almost to the muzzle of the piece, put it back again to take up the loose corns which were spilled by the way, and bring them back to the charge of powder. This done, the gunner must draw out his ladle and take out of the budge barrel a second ladleful, and so putting it in the piece up to the former ladleful, then you may draw it out and do as you did before, that no loose corns may lie in the bottom of the piece. And in drawing out his ladle, he must have a care that he let not fall any powder upon the ground; for it is a thing uncomely in a gunner to trample powder under feet. Then take a wisp of straw, hay or any other thing, and put it hard in at the mouth of the piece, then turn your ladle end for end to come to the rammer, thrust it into the piece after the wisp and drive it up with it, and it will carry all the loose corns which possibly may be scattered in the mould of the piece. Having driven the wad up to the powder give it two or three gentle shoves to make it lie close only, but drive it not too hard least you break your powder too much, which would hinder its force. The wisp or wad being close to the powder, draw out the rammer and put in the bullet... [and roll it] gently in the piece up to the wad that was before put in to keep up the powder. The shot being put in, put in a second wad after the bullet and thrust it also home to the bullet. Always remembering whilst the powder is putting in and wadding up, one be ready at the touch hole and keep it stopped with his thumb that no powder fly out at the touch hole, but that it be likewise filled with powder which may be supplied out of his powder horn.

Index

Bellingham, Sir Henry 71
Berkeley Castle 84
Berkhampstead 53
Berwick 22, 24, 42, 66, 67, 81
Besançon, Bishop of 26–7
Bigod, Hugh 41
Bingham, Colonel John 116
Birch, Colonel John 127–34, 172
Blackburn 83–4
Blake, Admiral Robert 96
Bletchingdon House, surrender of, 1645 98
blockades 31–5, 61–2, 69, 83, 105, 112, 138–9
boats 60, 68, 111
Bodiam Castle 21
Boniface of Savoy, Archbishop of Canterbury 61
Bonythion, Hannibal 137
Borthwick, Robert 75
Bosworth, battle of, 1485 66
Bothwell Castle, siege of 26
Bowes, Sir Robert 79
Bowyer, Captain Christopher 89–90
Boyle, Roger, Earl of Orrery 173–4
Boys, Colonel John 81
Brampton Bryan Castle, siege of, 1643 121–3, 123–4, 128
Brancepeth 67
brattices 20
Breauté, Falkes de 145–7
Breauté, William de 145
Brereton, Sir William 97, 99–100, 101, 102–8, 129
Breteuil, siege of, 1356 156–7
Brezé, Pierre de 68, 69
bribery 22, 39, 52, 67
Bridgwater, siege of, 1645 84, 124
Bristol 83, 84, 86, 89, 127, 127–8, 160
Brough Castle 191
Scottish capture of, 1274 26, 40
Bruce, Robert 23, 24, 147, 153
Bruce, The (Barbour) 153–5
Buckingham, Duke of, Henry Stafford 65
Burges, Colonel 98
Burgh, Hubert de 22, 46, 50, 52, 52–3, 54

Burghley, Lord 111
Butler, Colonel Robert 116
Byron, Sir John 97, 100, 102

Caernarfon 67
Caerphilly Castle 20
Calais 31
Caldecote Hall, defence of, 1642 120–1
Camden, William 99
camouflage, use of 24, 153
cannibalism 34, 35
cannon *see* artillery
Canterbury, Archbishop of, Boniface of Savoy 61
Carisbrooke Castle, siege of, 1377 19
Carlisle 22, 25, 28, 32, 36, 38, 39–40, 40, 48, 66, 67, 147–50, 150
Carlisle Castle 191
Carlton, Charles 85
Carolstein 29
Castle Rising 18
Chalus 19
Charles I, King 86, 95, 110–11, 123, 160
Charles II, King 134
Charles of Anjou 63
Charles of Navarre 156–7
Château Gaillard, siege of, 1203 35
Chester 97, 102, 103, 108, 124
Chester, Ranulf, Earl of 99
Cholmley, Sir Hugh 120
Civil War, the
    artillery types 81–2
    impact of gunpowder on 80–6
    number of sieges 85
    Pride's Purge 134
    women defenders during 111–18, 120–5
Clare, Gilbert de, Earl of Gloucester 57, 63
Clarendon, Earl of, Edward Hyde 140, 171
Clinton, Geoffrey de 18
coastal forts 80–1, 135
Colchester Castle 18
Collier, Thomas 108–9
Comynes, Philippe de 64

Further reading

The development of the English castle
Brown, R Allen 2004 *English Castles*, new ed. Woodbridge: Boydell Press
Colvin, H M, Brown, R A and Taylor, A J 1963 *The History of the King's Works: the Middle Ages*, 2 vols. London: HMSO
Fry, P Somerset 1980 *The David and Charles Book of Castles*. Newton Abbot: David & Charles
Gravett, C 2003 *Norman Stone Castles (1): The British Isles 1066–1216*. Oxford: Osprey
Morris, M 2003 *Castle*. London: Channel 4

Siege warfare in the Middle Ages
Beffeyte, R 2005 *L'art de la guerre au Moyen Age*. Rennes: Ouest-France
Bradbury, J 1992 *The Medieval Siege*. Woodbridge: Boydell Press
Bradbury, J 1996 *Stephen and Matilda: the Civil War of 1139–1153*. Stroud: Alan Sutton
Burl, A 2002 *God's Heretics: The Albigensian Crusade*. Stroud: Alan Sutton
Gravett, C 1990 *Medieval Siege Warfare*. London: Osprey
Giles, J A (transl) 1849 *Roger of Wendover's Flowers of History*, Vol II, Part II. London. (Llanerch Press facsimile reprint, 1996)
Maxwell, H (transl) 1913 *The Chronicle of Lanercost*. Glasgow. (Llanerch Press facsimile reprint, 2001)
Prawer, J 1972 *The Latin Kingdom of Jersusalem*. London: Weidenfeld & Nicolson
Prestwich, M 1996 *Armies and Warfare in the Middle Ages*. London, New Haven: Yale
Warner, P 1968 *Sieges of the Middle Ages*. London: Bell & Sons

Sieges in the north
Giles, J A (transl) 1849 *Roger of Wendover's Flowers of History*, Vol II, Part I. London. (Llanerch Press facsimile reprint, 1995)
Gillingham, J 2001 *The Angevin Empire*, 2nd ed. London: Arnold/OUP
Johnston, R C (ed) 1981 *Jordan Fantosme's Chronicle*. Oxford: Clarendon
Platt, C and McCarthy, M 1992 *Carlisle Castle guidebook*. London: English Heritage
Riley, H T (transl) 1853 *The Annals of Roger de Hoveden*, Vol I, Part II. London. (Llanerch Press facsimile reprint, 1995)
Salter, M 1997 *The Castles and Tower Houses of Northumberland*. Malvern: Folly Press
Saunders, S 1993 *Prudhoe Castle guidebook*. London: English Heritage
Stevenson, J 1856 *The History of William of Newburgh*. London. (Llanerch Press facsimile reprint, 1996)
Summerson, H 1999 'Brough Castle' in *Brougham Castle guidebook*. London: English Heritage

Rochester and Dover
Brown, R Allen 1986 *Rochester Castle guidebook*, 2nd ed. London: English Heritage
Carpenter, D A 1990 *The Minority of Henry III*. London: Methuen
Coad, J 1995 *The English Heritage book of Dover Castle*. London: Batsford
Giles, J A (transl) 1849 *Roger of Wendover's Flowers of History*, Vol II, Part II. London.
   (Llanerch Press facsimile reprint, 1996)
Goodall, J 2000 'Dover Castle and the Great Siege of 1216' in *Chateau Gaillard XIX: Actes du Colloque International de Graz, 1998*. Caen
Holt, J C 1992 *Magna Carta*, 2nd ed. Cambridge: CUP
Michel, F (ed) 1840 *Histoire des Ducs de Normandie et des Rois d'Angleterre*. Paris.
Warren, W L 1997 *King John*. London/New Haven: Yale

Kenilworth
Calendar of Liberate Rolls. 1916–64. London: HMSO
Halliwell, J O (ed) 1840 *The Chronicle of William de Rishanger of the Barons' Wars*. London:
   Camden Society
Kenilworth Historical Society (comp) 1966 *The Great Siege of Kenilworth 1266*. Kenilworth
Maddicott, J R 1994 *Simon de Montfort*. Cambridge: CUP
Morris, R K 2006 *Kenilworth Castle guidebook*. London: English Heritage
M C Prestwich 1998 *Edward I*. Berkeley

Alnwick, Bamburgh, Dunstanburgh
Giles, J A (ed) 1845 *The Chronicles of the White Rose of York*, 2 vols. London.
   (Llanerch Press facsimile reprint, 2004)
Gillingham, J 1981 *The Wars of the Roses: Peace and Conflict in 15th Century England*.
   London: Wiedenfeld & Nicolson
Haigh, P A 1995 *The Military Campaigns of the Wars of the Roses*. Stroud: Alan Sutton
Halliwell, J O (ed) 1839 *John Warkworth's Chronicle of the First Thirteen Years of the Reign of King Edward IV*. London. (Llanerch Press facsimile reprint, 1990)
Jones, M C E (transl) 1972 *Philippe de Comines. Memoirs*. Harmondsworth
Rose, R 2002 *Kings in the North: The House of Percy in British History*. London
Salter, M 1997 *The Castles and Tower Houses of Northumberland*. Malvern: Folly Press
Summerson, H 1993 *Dunstanburgh Castle guidebook*. London: English Heritage

Norham
Barr, N 2001 *Flodden 1513*. Stroud: Tempus
Duffy, C 1979 *Siege Warfare: The Fortress in the Early Modern World*, 1494–1660. London:
   Routledge
Ellis, H (ed) 1809 *Edward Hall's Chronicle*. London
Pearson, T and Ainsworth, S 2002 *Norham Castle*. English Heritage Archaeological
Investigation Report AI/25/2002. Swindon: English Heritage
Phillips, G 1999 *The Anglo-Scots Wars 1513–1550*. Woodbridge: Boydell Press
Saunders, A 1998 *Norham Castle guidebook*. London: English Heritage

The impact of gunpowder: siege warfare in the Civil War

Adair, J (ed) 1981 *They Saw it Happen: Contemporary Accounts of the Siege of Basing House*. Winchester

Carlton, C 1992 *Going to the Wars: The Experience of the British Civil Wars, 1638–1651*. London: Routledge

Firth, C H 1962 *Cromwell's Army, 3rd ed*. London: Methuen

Harrington, P 2003 *English Civil War Fortifications*. Oxford: Osprey

Harrington, P 2004 *English Civil War Archaeology*. London: Batsford

Young, P and Emberton, W 1978 *Sieges of the Great Civil War 1642–1646*. London: Bell & Hyman

Young, P and Holmes, R 1974 *The English Civil War*. London: Eyre Methuen

Wardour

Davison, B K 1999 *Old Wardour Castle guidebook*. London: English Heritage

Firth, C H (ed) 1894 *The Memoirs of Edmund Ludlow*, 2 vols. Oxford

MacLachlan, T 1997 *The Civil War in Wiltshire*. Salisbury: Rowan

Young, P 1981 *Civil War England*. Harlow: Longman

Beeston

Barratt, J 1995 *Civil War Stronghold: Beeston Castle at War*. Birkenhead: Caracole

Ellis, P (ed) 1993 *Beeston Castle, Cheshire: Excavations by Laurence Keen and Peter Hough*, 1968–85. London: English Heritage

Dore, R N 'Beeston Castle in the Great Civil War', *Transactions of the Lancashire and Cheshire Antiquarian Society*, 75–6 (1969), p103–22

Dore, R N (ed) 1984, 1990 *The letter books of William Brereton*, 2 vols. Chester: Record Society of Lancashire and Cheshire

Osborne, K 1995 *Beeston Castle guidebook*. London: English Heritage

Tucker, N 2003 *North Wales and Chester in the Civil War*, 2nd ed. Ashbourne: Landmark

Corfe

A True Relation of the Dorsetshire Affairs... and of the Late Siege of Corfe Castle in the Isle of Purbeck. London, 1643

'Mercurius Rusticus, the Country's Complaint, Recounting the Sad Events of this Unparraleld Warr', printed in Bond, T 1883 *History and Description of Corfe Castle in the Isle of Purbeck*. London

'Letters describing the final siege of Corfe', *Corfe Castle guidebook* Appendix IV. London: National Trust, 2003

Bankes, G 1853 *The Story of Corfe Castle*. London

Goodwin, T 1996 Dorset in the Civil War 1625–1665. Tiverton: Dorset Books

The Weaker Vessel?

Fraser, A 2002 *The Weaker Vessel: Woman's Lot in Seventeenth-century England*. London: Phoenix

Hudson, R 2000 *The Grand Quarrel: Women's Memoirs of the English Civil War*. Stroud: Sutton

Plowden, A 1998 *Women all on Fire: The Women of the English Civil War*. Stroud: Sutton

Goodrich

Heath-Agnew, E 1977 *Roundhead to Royalist, a biography of Colonel John Birch*. Hereford: Express Logic

Hutton, R 2003 *The Royalist War Effort*, 2nd ed. London: Routledge

Ashbee, J 2005 *Goodrich Castle guidebook*. London: English Heritage

Shoesmith, R 1995 *The Civil War in Hereford*. Woonton Almeley: Logaston Press

Webb, J and Webb, T W (eds) 1873 *Military Memoir of Colonel John Birch... written by Roe, his Secretary*. London

Pendennis

The Moderate Intelligencer No 77, August 1646

Coate, M 1963 *Cornwall in the Great Civil War and Interregnum*, 2nd ed. Truro: Bradford Barton

Linzey, R 2002 *The Castles of Pendennis and St Mawes, guidebook*. London: English Heritage

Oliver, S P 1875 *Pendennis and St Mawes: an historical sketch of two Cornish castles*. London. (Cornish Publications facsimile edition, 1984)

Sprigge, J 1647 *Anglia Rediviva: England's Recovery*. London. (Ken Trotman facsimile edition, 1984)

Young, P 1981 *Civil War England*. Harlow: Longman

Appendices

I Johnson R C (ed) 1981 *Jordan Fantosme's Chronicle*. Oxford: OUP

II Giles J A (transl) 1849 *Roger of Wendover's Flowers of History, Vol II, Part II*. London: Bohn

III Maxwell H (ed) 1913 *The Chronicle of Lanercost*. Glasgow: MacLehose

IV *Calendar of Liberate Rolls*, 1916–64. London: HMSO

V Eyre-Todd G (transl) 1996 *The Bruce*. Edinburgh: Mercat (facsimile of 1907 edition)

VI Brereton G (transl) 1978 *John Froissart: Chronicles*. London: Penguin

VII Cruso J 1632 *Militarie Instructions for the Cavallrie*. Cambridge: CUP

IX Hutchinson, L *Memoirs of the Life of Colonel Hutchinson*. London: Everyman

X Oliver S P 1984 *Pendennis and St Mawes*. Redruth: Cornish Publications (facsimile of 1875 edition)

XI Webb J and Webb T W (eds) 1873 *Military Memoir of Colonel John Birch... written by Roe, his Secretary*. London: Camden Society

XII Boyle R 1677 *A Treatise of the Art of War*. London: Henry Herringman

XIII Robins J 1742 *New Principles of Gunnery*. London: J Nourse

Places to visit

As well as being an enjoyable day out in itself, a visit to the castles mentioned in this book will really help to understand the events described. Needless to say, due to destruction during the sieges themselves, later additions and rebuilding, or even deliberate demolition or 'slighting', many of these castles have changed considerably since the time they were besieged. Even in these cases, though, a visit will still help to underline the importance of the castle's location and its strengths and weaknesses during the siege. The majority of the castles listed below are in the care of English Heritage and further information about facilities, opening hours, access and parking can be found on their website at www.english-heritage.org.uk.

Alnwick Castle, Northumberland (Duke of Northumberland)
In Alnwick town centre. Tel: 01665 510777
After Windsor, Alnwick is the second-largest inhabited castle in England. Its extensive gardens and use as a location for the Harry Potter films have made it one of the region's busiest tourist attractions. Much of the castle was restored in the 19th century but its main gatehouse is a superb example of 14th-century military architecture.

Bamburgh Castle, Northumberland (Trustees of Lord Armstrong)
Off the A1, 6miles east of Belford on B1342. Tel: 01668 214515
Extensive restorations in the 18th and 19th centuries mean that the most notable survivors of the siege of 1464 are the outer gatehouse and Norman keep. Perched on a rocky outcrop overlooking the sea, Bamburgh occupies one of the most spectacular locations for a castle in England and it is easy to see why it was considered so strong.

Bedford Castle, Bedfordshire (Bedford Council Council)
In Bedford town centre. Tel: 01234 353323 (Bedford Museum)
Bedford castle was largely demolished after its capture in 1224 in order to prevent it again being used as a centre of opposition to royal power. The surviving castle mound has recently undergone an award-winning facelift and the nearby Bedford Museum houses a new exhibition about the castle.

Beeston Castle, Cheshire (EH)
11 miles south-east of Chester on minor road off A49. Tel: 01244 412111
Beeston has perhaps the most stunning views of any castle in England. It was slighted at the end of the Civil War but the inner bailey gatehouse still survives, together with part of the outer wall with a number of open-backed towers. Alterations to loopholes made during the Civil War are visible.

Brough Castle, Cumbria (EH)
Off A66, 8 miles south-east of Appleby. Tel: 0191 269 1227
Built on the site of a Roman fort, Brough was one of the first stone castles to be constructed in England. Some of its original herringbone masonry can still be seen. The present tower keep was built in about 1200 to replace the one destroyed by William the Lion in 1174.

Carlisle Castle, Cumbria (EH)
In Carlisle city centre. Tel: 01228 625600
Carlisle's key position on the western end of the Scottish border meant the defences of its castle have been frequently updated. Although subsequently altered, the keep and inner and outer gatehouses date back to the sieges of 1174 and 1315. The keep houses exhibitions about the castle's history.

Corfe Castle, Dorset (NT)
In Corfe Castle village, 5 miles south-east of Wareham. Tel: 01929 481294
Although Corfe was extensively slighted after its capture, enough of its defences remain to give an impression of the original strength of the place. One of the trenches dug by the sappers trying to demolish the castle is still visible. The Rings, the medieval earthwork where the Parliamentarians sited their guns during their first siege of the castle, is a 400yd walk away.

Dover Castle, Kent (EH)
On the east side of Dover, off the A2. Tel: 01304 211067
Dover is one of England's greatest castles. Its medieval walls are largely intact although they were later cut down in size in order to house artillery. It is possible to explore a medieval tunnel which leads out under the blocked north towers while a triangular outwork to the north of the castle marks the position of the barbican captured by the French. The basement of the 12th-century keep houses an audio-visual display about the events of 1216 while a reconstruction trebuchet stands in the inner bailey.

Dunstanburgh Castle, Northumberland (EH)
8 miles north-east of Alnwick, on footpath from Craster or Embleton. Tel: 01665 576231
The best way to approach Dunstanburgh is along the coastal path from Craster. Even in its ruinous state the castle's enormous gatehouse still dominates the approach. By the time of the Wars of the Roses it had been blocked and turned into a keep.

Goodrich Castle, Herefordshire (EH)
5 miles south of Ross-on-Wye, off the A40. Tel: 01600 890538
Even though many of its towers are roofless and the damage caused by Birch's siege artillery is plain to see, much of the fabric of this compact and powerful castle remains intact. Roaring Meg, the mortar that caused so much destruction in 1646, is now housed inside its walls.

Kenilworth Castle, Warwickshire (EH)
In Kenilworth town centre. Tel: 01926 864152
One side of Kenilworth's impressive keep, which was altered in the 16th century, was demolished during the castle's post Civil War slighting. Although the lake around the castle has been drained the area it once covered is clearly visible. A number of stone balls, presumably from the siege of 1266, can be seen in the castle grounds.

Norham Castle, Northumberland (EH)
7 miles south-west of Berwick, off the B6470. Tel: 01289 304493
Norham was extensively rebuilt after the damage it suffered during the siege of 1513 but the keep and eastern part of the original curtain wall still remain. Sixteenth-century earthworks are clearly visible to the south of the castle.

Pendennis Castle, Cornwall (EH)
On Pendennis Head, 1 mile south-east of Falmouth. Tel: 01747 870487
Pendennis's important strategic position meant that it remained in military use for over 400 years and its defences were frequently extended and upgraded. The Henrician castle and Tudor ramparts are still intact while the positions of the earthworks built to the north-west are marked by low grassy banks.

Prudhoe Castle, Northumberland (EH)
On minor road off the A695. Tel: 01661 833459
Although considerably altered, Prudhoe's 12th-century gatehouse and keep still survive. The 19th-century manor house built inside its walls houses an exhibition detailing the history of the castle.

Rochester Castle, Kent (EH)
Of the A2 by Rochester Bridge. Tel: 01634 402276
Much of Rochester's original curtain wall has either been built over or destroyed. However its keep still stands, including the circular tower built to replace the one brought down by John's miners in 1215.

Wardour Castle, Wiltshire (EH)
Off the A30, 2 miles south-west of Tisbury. Tel: 01747 870487
Old Wardour Castle is now surrounded by picturesque parkland but evidence of the siege of 1644 can be seen in the bullet marks around many of its windows and its collapsed masonry, brought down by the accidental explosion of the Royalist mine.